MW00632760

cultivate

cul·ti·vate \ˈkəl-tə-ˌvāt\

: to prepare and use for the raising of crops
: to loosen or break up the soil
: to foster the growth of
: to improve by labor, care or study
: further, encourage
: to seek the society of
: make friends with

a note to the reader

In these pages you will find recipes for spending time with the Lord and be prompted to journal His voice. Jesus says in John 10:27, "My sheep hear my voice, and I know them, and they follow me" (ESV). As a child of God, you know His voice; you hear Him, and it is important that you record, savor and declare His thoughts over your life. By recording His thoughts, you will remember how deeply He loves you and who you truly are. We encourage you to center your heart in this simple truth: God is a loving Father, ready and eager to speak to you. It is our hope that through these pages, you will be inspired to draw close to Him and the people He has put in your life. Be courageous! It is in this process that our minds are transformed and we are able to live confidently as His sons and daughters.

a note from the artists

We work on fifty acres of forest, thick and full of oaks, maples, cedars, beech and birch trees, all that grow in circles—rings within rings of wood. Each tree is forever marked with beauty and pain. If they could speak, they would say, "We are going somewhere but have miraculously stayed rooted." In planning the visual content for this book, we were moved to capture the essence of what surrounds us everyday: circles. Circles speak of covenant and closeness. They lack rigid edges and strong lines, carrying consistency and movement. We have included prints from trees that have fallen on our land, old and young, along with our own exploration of this moving and eternal shape. We hope that you feel met by the art in this volume and that with each circle, you are inspired to soften the edges of your heart and give in to growth.

the art of connection

Opening Thoughts by Melissa Helser

We were all made for connection. Connection simply means "to join two or more things, sometimes for the same cause, origin or goal." Humanity is hardwired to need each other. From the beginning of time, God understood that it is not good for us to be alone. He reached inside the "man" He created and separated him into two. He essentially said that communion with Him is not enough, that He wants us to have fellowship with one another. He created us to need connection.

Connection takes time and work. It isn't easy. It requires an understanding of self and others. It requires more than good theories. It demands practice in everyday life. Just when we think we're done learning, another conflict or misunderstanding arises and we have to go the distance again. Connection asks us to go beyond what is easy and comfortable, reach outside of our own tendencies and learn humanity. Connection says that we are worth being loved, and so are our spouses, parents, children and friends. Connection is impossible if we remain rigid and unwilling to grow.

As of April 2018, I have been married eighteen years to a glorious introvert. I would definitely say that I am an extrovert and our kids are one of each. I have had to learn and grow. I have had to give in to asking questions, seeking to understand myself and the people I love the most. I have twenty staff, each one different in personality, story and life experience. I have had to give in to knowing them and loving them beyond what is easy for me. Connection says, "I am willing to be wrong and seek to understand. I am willing to learn a new way in order to really know you. I am willing to lay down 'my way' in order to communicate value to your heart."

In the last seven years, Jonathan and I have fallen in love with emotional health. We, along with our whole staff, have given in to the deep process of growth and the brutal honesty with self that emotional health requires. We have humbled our hearts to receive from teachers unlike ourselves. We have read and re-read, and we have practiced...A LOT. We have practiced Mark 12:30 over and over: "'Love the Lord your God with all your heart and with all your soul and with all your mind and with all your strength.' The second is this: 'Love your neighbor as yourself'"(NIV). We have chosen to fall into the arms of a loving Father in tension, and we have fought for beautiful confrontation and resolve, encouragement and celebration. The fruit of this practice is the Cageless Birds community. Many people have asked us to write a book on community, but instead we have decided to reflect on healthy connection because that is what creates a powerful community.

A friend once said to Jonathan and me, "Don't try to reproduce your model. You can only reproduce values. Figure out what your values really are." We took that to heart and have spent the last seven years pressing into our value system, not just so we can run great schools and do fruitful ministry, but so that we can thrive in the 95% of life: in our marriage, in parenthood, as friends and as co-laborers in the Kingdom.

In Volume V we chose to focus on the immediate family: parents, spouses, children. Jonathan and I have given our lives to walking out a healthy marriage, raising our children led by the Holy Spirit and discipling young adults to do the same. We couldn't talk about Kingdom family without talking about what we've invested in our immediate family. Each person in Kingdom family has a unique story and a powerful opportunity to transform his or her legacy. We work out our salvation by loving God, loving ourselves and loving people. In Volume VI we will venture into the conversation about Kingdom family, but we want to begin this conversation by addressing some of the most foundational relationships in many of our lives.

We recognize that not every section of this book will directly relate to the season of life that every person is in. Not everyone is in a season of dating, and not everyone is married. Many don't have children, and others have lost parents. Regardless of the season you are in, our hope is that this volume will inspire you to open up both your history and your future to the Lord. You are a significant placeholder in your lineage, and it is vital that you open up dialogue about what it looks like for you to affect your immediate family.

This volume is meant to give testimony of real people failing and learning and leaning into the Holy Spirit for help. It is not a compilation of articles and interviews with perfect people; better yet, it is a collection of words and stories and imagery from people yielded to the process. We pray you feel inspired, challenged, liberated. And mostly that you feel permission to pursue the hard work of connection—that through it all, in both the big and the small moments, life would become beautiful.

01. COVENANT

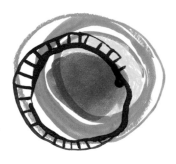

02. PURSUIT

03. LEGACY

04. HONOR

COVENANT

CULTIVATING AN INTENTIONAL MARRIAGE

"So they are no longer two, but one flesh.
Therefore what God has joined together,
let no one separate."   Matthew 19:6

CEDAR
cut from the woods of Sophia, NC
approx. 70 years old

A BIG YES

Recipe for Dreaming into Your Marriage ——— Jonathan David Helser

Artwork ——— Morgan Campbell

One of the greatest compliments I have been given came from a sixteen-year-old boy after one of our album release concerts. The one thing this young man wanted for his birthday was to come to our concert. His parents surprised him and drove him six hours to attend. Later, his parents told us that on their long drive back, there was one thing their son could not stop talking about from the night. It wasn't the lights or sound system; the band or the songs we had written. What he couldn't stop talking about was the way that I affectionately looked across the stage at Melissa during the night. He told his mom and dad that this was the kind of husband he wanted to be one day. What he said moved me and brought back a rush of memories. Suddenly, I was caught up in what it felt like to be a sixteen-year-old boy, inspired by the marriages I saw around me.

I remember as a young boy watching the way my father loved and romanced my mother. It awakened a dream inside of me to one day become a husband. From the way he would wrap his arms around her when he came home from work, to the way he would search for the perfect gift each Christmas, and to all the normal moments of life when I watched him love my mother with his whole heart. I couldn't wait to one day love my wife like that. This dream that formed in my heart as a young boy became like a rudder to help me navigate through the temptations of my youth. My teenage years were not perfect, but I can look back on those days and see that what empowered me to say "no" to the pull of the world was the "yes" in my heart to one day be a husband. Even in my youth, I had my eyes set on the reward of marriage. When we cultivate a big yes, we have the power to say no.

Now as a father, I am on the other side of this story. I have two children who have grown up so fast. Just the other day my fifteen-year-old son said to me, "Dad, I can't wait to be a husband one day. It's got to be the greatest thing in the world. It's like getting to have a sleepover with your best friend every night." I didn't have to convince my son that marriage is amazing. He has been watching me fall deeper in love with his mother since the day he was born. He knows more than anyone that we are not perfect. He sees us on our best and our worst days, yet he daily sees the reward of marriage. Our marriage is one of the loudest messages we will ever preach to our kids. One of my goals as a father is to make marriage the most irresistible and contagious choice for them.

I am eighteen years into this beautiful journey called marriage and I am still dreaming of the marriage I want to have. I still get so inspired being around other marriages that are thriving and learning from the way they love one another. When I'm around those marriages, I try to pay attention. I practice asking the Father, "What is it about that couple that's so amazing? What is it about them that is inspiring me?" Letting the love of other couples affect me is a way of investing into my own marriage. In each season I am learning about the beautiful gift of marriage, and each day I am getting to put it to practice. In the Kingdom, we never arrive. God is eternal and there is no end to Him. There is always more. Those who are close to God never stop dreaming. Whether you have been married for forty years or four months, there is always much more your Father has for you.

Prompt: Take a few moments to be still and then ask the Holy Spirit to bring to your remembrance a few marriages that have inspired you. Write down the names of those families and then reflect on the specific qualities in those marriages that have spoken to your heart. As you remember specific things in these marriages that have resonated with you, write them. Once you finish jotting down a few things for each family, take some time and dream about what these qualities would look like in your own marriage. If you are single, dream about what these qualities would look like in your future marriage. Now intentionally ask God for those dreams to begin to grow and be fulfilled in your life.

- Kindness/gentleness
- loyalty/endurance

11

EVERY DAY

FORGIVE NESS

Recipe Series on Practicing Forgiveness ——— Pete & Sammy Greig

Photography ——— Personal Collection

turning toward

Pete Greig

My wife, Sammy, and I were sitting together on the sofa in our home, hunched comfortably into each other's bodies. It was the twenty-third anniversary of our wedding day, and we were flicking through an old, red scrapbook. Finding the page where our vows were glued back in 1994, we took turns renewing them for the twenty-third time, quietly thanking God for helping us stay true and repenting wherever we'd failed in the previous year. On that rainy wedding day, almost a quarter of a century ago, we had solemnly promised to "keep short accounts"—to apologize quickly. We had no idea how big a deal that was going to be. Sammy and I have wiped the slate clean so often in our marriage, it's a wonder there's any slate left.

I wish people were more honest about covenant relationship. Yes, marriage is glorious and wonderful and beautiful, but it is also the hardest thing ever. I never realized just how selfish I could be until I got married. I remember telling someone once when I was single that I couldn't recall ever having lost my temper. But then I got married. And then we had kids. In marriage, we discover the very best and the very worst of ourselves. Its delights are many, but marriage also turns out to be Christ's favored crucible for character formation.

The Gottman Institute in New York studies marriage to discover why some survive and so many falter. Successful marriages can be predicted with a 94% accuracy rate through a certain factor. In healthy relationships spouses continually "turn toward" one another. Turning toward for me might mean that if Sammy says, "I like this song," instead of grunting distractedly or disagreeing, I reciprocate positively with questions and kindness. Or if Sammy says, "I'm exhausted," I avoid responding with a passive "Me too" or a dismissive "Why don't you go to bed?" but instead reply with empathy and concern. Turning toward Sammy in this way creates a climate of grace in our home. If I claim to have forgiven her but remain moody, distant or passive-aggressive, I'm playing power games. On average, partners in healthy marriages turn toward one another in these kinds of ways 87% of the time. It's as simple as that.

Sammy and I argued one day, and I stormed out of the house. Furious, I walked around the woods near our home telling the trees all the reasons why she was wrong and I was right. But as the light faded, so did my indignation. I began to realize what an idiot I'd been. And so, with my tail between my legs, I made my way home wondering how angry she would be and what words I should choose to make it right. At the door Sammy welcomed me with an unexpected smile. I tried to say sorry, but she just took my hand and led me to the kitchen where she'd been making my favorite food. She had turned toward me with a smile, with a touch, with an act of kindness. The storm was past, and we were still standing. Somewhere underground our roots intertwined a little more.

Prompt: Whether you're married, dating or single, pray slowly through this brilliant, ancient relationship advice from the apostle Paul: "Love from the center of who you are; don't fake it. Run for dear life from evil; hold on for dear life to good. Be good friends who love deeply; practice playing second fiddle. Don't burn out; keep yourselves fueled and aflame" (Romans 12: 9-11, MSG). Think through Paul's words, and audit your heart. Ask yourself, "Have I been 'turning toward' my best friend recently or subtly pulling away? How might I dominate less so I can 'play second fiddle' today? From which current temptations do I need to 'run for dear life'? By what means of grace might I keep covenant commitment 'fueled and aflame' this week?" Pray, and journal the Lord's voice.

Love Covers

Sammy Greig

Grace is a mystery I've been trying to understand my entire life. Growing up in a family culture of conflict, I was often banished to my bedroom in disgrace. Eventually I found a key that unlocked my bedroom door, granting me access back to the family. It was a simple, single, magic word: sorry. I would write it on scraps of paper and drop it down through the bannisters for my parents to find. I would say it even when it wasn't my fault. Sometimes I would scream it in defiance, though I didn't know why. I didn't realize how much of that childhood baggage I would bring into my marriage.

When I eventually heard the Gospel and gave my life to Jesus as a young adult, my experience seemed to re-enforce that same transactional view of apology and absolution with which I had been raised: "All you have to do is say sorry," the preacher said. "Admit your sins to the Father, and you'll be forgiven." It was a familiar formula, and so I did it. I whispered that magic word once again and stepped out of my bedroom, only this time into the family of God.

I may not have fully understood the way repentance works, but my newfound relationship with Jesus began to change everything. My entire extended family soon became Christians too, but the journey of transformation as a relational reality rather than a transactional one was to be long and slow. In fact, it was probably only when I married Pete that I really began to understand grace.

When things weren't perfect in our marriage—and of course they often weren't—I would always instinctively seek to allocate blame and extricate an apology. This seemed more important to me than simply being kind, and of course, it invariably escalated conflict. In those harsh, early days, Pete and I often quoted, "Speak the truth in love," (Ephesians 4:15, NIV) but ignored, "Above all, love each other deeply because love covers over a multitude of sins" (I Peter 4:8, NIV). The slightest sin was confronted, never covered.

Having kids made sense of grace at last. As a parent you find yourself unimpressed by formulae, inclined to forgive. An apology is often not necessary. A hug will do. Or a few tears. Or even a cheeky grin. I've learned to let most things go and not to take offense so easily. To confront and request a 'sorry' only when it is absolutely necessary for my child's own sake. Like the time the hamster escaped under the floorboards in our oldest son's bedroom. He tried to retrieve her by cutting a large square of carpet from the middle of his room. I was cross to say the least. The hamster had cost us $5; the carpet would cost hundreds to replace. God helped me not to yell, but to listen—to understand that Huddy wasn't being naughty by cutting the carpet but caring toward his hamster. That night we rearranged his bedroom to cover the hole in the carpet. We never did find the hamster, but instead of arguing we came closer than ever in a world where people (and even hamsters) matter more than mere things. After twenty-five years of marriage, Pete and I still get it wrong sometimes, but we are softer these days. As a result, our relationship is stronger and happier. We love each other more now than when we walked down the aisle, and we are confronting less and covering each other more with a warm blanket of grace.

Prompt: What have you learned about grace and forgiveness from your family culture? Is it in line with God's heart and His word? Pray this simple prayer and journal what the Lord says to you: "Father, thank you that you come running toward me in love even before I've managed to say sorry. Teach me to walk in greater forgiveness, and grant me a glimpse of your compassion for those who offend me. Help me to run toward them this week with expressions of your amazing grace."

We are confronting less and
covering each other more
with a warm blanket of grace.

Fifty Year Love

An Interview on Staying in Love for a Lifetime with Ken & Linda Helser

By Allie Sampson & Erin Gravitt / Photography from Personal Collection & Sydnee Mela

Crisp February air cuts a path through the trees as we climb the familiar trail to Ken and Linda's home. I can't think of a more appropriate couple to interview on Valentine's Day. Ken and Linda Helser are the patriarch and matriarch of this community, and they've offered a stunning example of steadfast friendship and love. It's common to see them walking the land together hand-in-hand, cutting jokes and laughing as their little dog, Ollie, chases them across the field. Fifty-two years into marriage, their friendship is tangible. Every student or guest who comes to A Place for the Heart ends up commenting, "Ken and Linda are just so in love!"

Sunshine pours through the windows of their sunroom and laughter permeates our conversation, Linda giggling as Ken teases her. Ken serves us fresh cups of coffee while Linda pulls black and white photographs out of a manila folder. "They were my grandparents," she smiles, extending the print of Ken and her surrounded by family on their wedding day. These were the ones who went before them, modeling commitment and resilient love. This walked-out commitment would mark Ken and Linda's lives and make way for them to become people who believe in the power of covenant. As you read their story, may you find yourself inspired to love deeply and feel a fresh hope in the power of commitment.

THE TWO OF YOU ARE STILL SO IN LOVE WITH ONE ANOTHER— SOMETHING REALLY RARE TO SEE THESE DAYS. HOW HAVE YOU STAYED IN LOVE FOR ALMOST 52 YEARS?

LINDA: I think one of the things that has helped us stay in love is trust. We really trust each other. That doesn't just happen. It takes time. Ken knows my weakest places and my strongest places. I'm not afraid for him to come to the weakest areas of my life, because I trust that the reason he's going to those areas is because he wants them to become my strongest areas. He always says to me, "You can't turn your back to fear, you've got to walk toward it." He helps push me to those areas I'm afraid of because it's the only way I'm going to get rid of that fear. It's hard to trust somebody that much. We always want everyone to see our good points. We don't like for them to see those weak areas—sometimes they're embarrassing. Ken

and I have had some conversations that had the potential to be hurtful. They're embarrassing.

I remember one time when we were in Chicago at a really nice restaurant with some friends. Ken was telling a story, and I kept interrupting him. He's not so good with keeping the details in retelling a moment, and sometimes he talks in extremes. I kept interrupting him because he wasn't telling it exactly right. After the story was told—along with my twenty interruptions—he whispered to me where no one else could hear, "When you do that, it makes me feel so foolish." Because of the trust we have for each other I knew he wasn't mad with me. He was letting me know that hurt. And it hurt me so bad that I had done that to him, but I knew he was right. I should not have done that, because it was embarrassing to him.

We've had times of going to the hurtful things in our marriage instead of shying away from them. There've been a lot of times with Ken where I see that he's injuring himself because of the way that he feels about something. I can't stand it because I know he's hurting himself, and I want him to have the best of the best. Sometimes we won't go to the painful areas with somebody because we don't want to make them feel bad. I recently looked up the word trust, and one of the words it's associated with is confidence. I think Ken has given me so much confidence in who I am because of the way he trusts me and believes in me. Trust has played a huge part in our marriage. Learning to trust each other began with learning to trust God. By trusting Him with our life, we learned how to trust each other. I think that's a huge part of why things have worked.

KEN: In the beginning, you're so in love, so starry-eyed, you think that love will be able to get you past all the hard things in life. You think, "Love never fails," but "Love never fails" is only powerful when love is attacked by all the forces of hell, because that's how you learn: "Wow. This love *really* never fails." One of the great quotes about love and marriage is from my son. He said to me, before he married Melissa, "Daddy, I'm seeing something about marriage. Real Christian marriage is not falling in love with each other. It's falling into God with each other." When you fall into God with someone, you have to work it out. If I were to walk

away from love, I would be walking away from God. The covenant is everything because you made a covenant before God. "Till death do us part, in sickness and in health—in everything that is going to come against us…I am not going to leave you." That's where love grows. Love grows from overcoming. Our love grew through conflict, because conflict is the price we pay for intimacy. When there's conflict, it hurts so bad that you have to resolve it, and that is where you overcome.

The breakdown of marriage is when there is compassion fatigue. It's where you become numb and lose compassion—that is the picture of marriage today. People decide, "It's not worth it. I'm tired. I don't feel like going through it." And that's what happens in marriage. We get compassion fatigue and then we just keep numbing things down.

DID YOU ALL EVER FIND COMPASSION FATIGUE IN YOUR 52 YEARS?

KEN: We could have. But we found that our marriage was worth fighting for. Linda says, "In the end of this life, we are the summation of our choices." And there comes a point when we choose to love each other because we realize it's worth fighting for.

WHERE DID YOUR VIEWS OF COMMITMENT AND MARRIAGE COME FROM?

LINDA: When we got married, we didn't have marriage counseling. Pastors only met with you to find out how you wanted the wedding ceremony to be. Then when we became Christians, we were one of the few couples that were married in our friend groups, so of course we didn't get counseling from our friends. We thought back about it, but we never really got any words of advice. Nobody

> In the end of this life, we are the summation of our choices. And there comes a point when we choose to love each other because we realize it's worth fighting for.

sat down with us and talked to us about marriage. So when I think back to where my views of marriage came from, it came from my parents and grandparents. It didn't come from them saying anything. Their comitment was so strong.

KEN: Linda and I had wonderful parents and grandparents. Both of us had grandparents that were farmers and we grew up seeing how they lived. They had hard lives, but there was no doubt about commitment. Whether Linda and I knew it or not, we wanted that commitment. It subconsciously got inside of us.

When we came to Christ, He was always counseling us. One of the things we began to notice as baby Christians was that we weren't great at praying together—I felt like such a hypocrite in front of her—but whenever we'd have discussions with each other about important things, when we'd finish we'd say, "Oh, that was prayer because Jesus just sat here with us." Putting things out on the table in front of each other was almost like prayer and we felt like we could say amen at the end of it. And that continues to this day.

CAN YOU RECALL A MOMENT WHERE THE HOLY SPIRIT COUNSELED YOU IN YOUR MARRIAGE?

KEN: For me in my life, there was a time that was one of the greatest moments of learning Linda (as a baby Christian) and seeing what an incredible gift she was. There was something that she wanted me to do and I was busy with something else and I was harsh. There's a Scripture that instructs husbands to be considerate, honoring and respectful of their wives "so that nothing will hinder your prayers," (I Peter 3:7, NIV). I realized that when I got out of sorts with her, God didn't hear my prayers. The only way I could get back in relationship with God was to get back in relationship with Linda.

Now that counsel is everything. I was harsh and I went back downstairs to talk to the Lord. It was like He wasn't even there. I said to Him, "I know. You're gone. You're not even going to listen to a word I'm saying until I go make it right." I went trudging up the stairs and I went over to the sink where Linda was standing. I knew she'd been crying and I begged her to leave the dishes and come with me to the living room. I put my arms around her—she was so mad, I might as well have been hugging a statue—and while we were standing there the Lord said, "You pray, you read, you fast, you do all the disciplines, you go to meetings, you don't get in the car without listening to a teaching. Your wife knows about 10% of what you know about me but she's a godly woman, because she loves her family. The measuring stick for godliness is not how much she knows, but how well she loves her family, and she loves you."

In that moment, my wife, who didn't know a whole lot theologically, became a spiritual giant in my eyes. I realized I knew a lot about God, but she *knew* God. That changed my view of everything about her. It is important, in love, for you to have God's perspective of the person. He gave you that person as a gift and you will not abuse God's gift. For love to continue to grow, you have to have a revelation and a viewpoint of the gift God's given you. You don't just decide you're going to love—romantic love runs out. If God's not there when the love runs out, you end up with compassion fatigue. When you wear out of something, it's because you're doing it on your own and God's not in it. Try having a marriage without God; it's an absolute disaster. You can't love someone without God, because God is Love. My ability to love Linda is God.

WHAT'S BEEN YOUR FAVORITE MEMORY IN YOUR 52 YEARS OF MARRIAGE—A MOMENT WHERE YOU REALIZED GOD GAVE YOU A REALLY GOOD GIFT?

LINDA: We both agree this memory is our favorite, even though it's kind of unusual. Six or seven years ago, Ken had to go through a six-week cancer treatment in Jacksonville, Florida. He went down early to find us a place to stay, and just like Jesus, through crazy events, a lady gave us a place for free right on the St. Johns River. I was so excited that we'd have four weeks, just the two of us. That is until we got close to our apartment and Ken began to prepare me that the place was not all that hot. He said it wasn't in the most desirable neighborhood, and perhaps we might have to look for another place… Well, it was worse than he had prepared me for. It was a drab, prison-gray, three-story apartment lined with plastic flowers that obviously had been leftovers from cemetery arrangements. No. It was not exactly plush. It was tiny and overcrowded with furniture, and as soon as we got my things out of the car, Ken had to go get his treatment. I stayed behind to unpack and I'd brought a few things from home. At first, I thought, *Oh my gosh, you could get really depressed in this place.* And then I thought, *Oh Lord, I'm sorry. We've been given this free place to stay for a month and here I am complaining about it.* I said, "Okay God, you and I've got to get to work." I took off the bedspread that looked like it was from the 1940s. By the time Ken got back I'd completely changed it—it didn't look like the same place anymore. He couldn't believe it when he came in. I cooked a new recipe for supper that night. He'd been so proud of himself because before I'd gotten there, he'd been cooking all

his meals on his own. He took the first bite and started crying. He said, "You know, I thought I was doing pretty good on my own, but it's different with you here." That was the beginning of one of the most incredible months we've had in our marriage. Never in our lives were we in a place where it was just us. There wasn't anybody else—no kids, no grandkids. We'd get calls from them, but everyday was our day, except his two-hour treatment time. It became this real adventure. We'd take walks. We got library cards and checked out books and DVDs. We found the local farmer's market and we'd go and pick up fish at night to cook in our little apartment. It was the most romantic time. On weekends we'd discover new places we could go and we met some incredible people. It was just us! It felt like no one else existed but the two of us, and we'd never had that before. We had children so quickly after we were married, we never really had the time just the two of us with no plans. I thought about it later and I said, "It's amazing because you have these couples

who have been married for years and when the husbands retire the wives think, *Oh gosh, what am I going to do with him all day long?* And actually, we thoroughly enjoy each other from morning to night." We want to do it again—not the cancer, but having that time just the two of us. We really had the best time of our lives.

WHAT'S YOUR FAVORITE THING ABOUT BEING MARRIED?

KEN: One thing I really love about being married to her is she knows I'm an introvert and she gives me space. When we get up in the mornings, I have the coffee ready for her and then I go downstairs. We both have about an hour and a half with the Lord before we have time with each other. So when we do have time with each other, we've first been with Him. Not everybody can do that. Some people have young kids and schedules. It's only in the last couple of years that we've been able to do that.

LINDA: My favorite thing about being married is having someone who is my very best friend. I get to get up every morning and know that we have a day together. That sounds cheesy, but it's true. We either get to do the day together or we come back together at the end of the day and there's somebody there that cares about what happened to you that day.

KEN: Even if it's been a very difficult or sad day, you have someone to share the burden with. If anyone ever says to me, "I want to tell you something, but you can't tell anyone," I tell them, "Don't tell me because I will tell my wife." There are no more secrets. When you have intimacy with a person you share everything. You share your burdens with one another, and to have somebody to share that with is just the greatest joy.

WHAT WOULD YOU SAY TO COUPLES WHO WANT TO GET MARRIED AND STAY IN LOVE FOR THE LONG HAUL, BUT ARE NERVOUS ABOUT "MAKING IT WORK"?

LINDA: It's hard because everything around you is telling you you can't make it. I can understand why there's this real hesitation around marriage—the fear of not wanting to go through a failed marriage. But in anything it takes both parties. You've got two people and they choose to love each other. They make the choice that there is no other choice. You go into it making the choice that this is it, and you choose to love that person for the rest of your life. Ken always tells people when we're doing marriage counseling, "If you knew you were going away to live on the mission field and you knew that once you got there you'd never be able to come back to your home, you would pray about that long and hard, wouldn't you? Marriage is an even greater decision than that is. You need to pray about it and not just jump into it." Ask yourself: *Do I want to make that commitment to this person?*

KEN: Be certain that marrying that person is the will of God for your life. If you know that the will of God for your life is to get married to someone, then you won't walk away from them because you know that to walk away from that person is to walk away from the will of God. The will of God is more powerful than that person.

Conflict

Recipe for Identifying Your Needs in Conflict

Writing & Artwork ——— *Justina Stevens*

We were really young when we fell in love. Jake had this way of looking in my eyes and helping me feel like the most understood person in the world. He was, and still is, an amazing listener who gave me space when I would rummage through sentences trying to find explanations and ideas. When we married, we were both sure we were just alike: similar ways of processing, an adoration for the quiet, with the same quirky likes and dislikes. Three years of dating behind us had strengthened our friendship and heightened our longing to build a home.

Once we were man and wife, to my surprise I realized how different we actually were. We didn't process the same; he needed space to talk things out and feel validated, and I needed to be alone in a quiet room. We didn't decompress the same; he needed adventure, and I needed time to rest. We didn't engage community the same; I wanted to stay at home and have a couple of guests over for dinner, and he wanted to sit around a fire until two in the morning talking with his friends. Our needs clashed. The more we tried to solve the puzzle of who-needs-what, our irritations rose. To make matters trickier, I dealt with severe chronic pain from a car accident in the first year of our marriage, which only added to our newfound tension. Neither of us intended for my pain to trump whose needs got met, but sometimes it did. Jake felt inclined to stay home, to be present for me, even if it would have been wiser to do separate things. We were so in love and so irritated with each other.

We fought. We raised our voices. We didn't like what we were doing, but with unmet needs we found ourselves floundering. Jonathan and Melissa always said in marriage counseling, "Tension makes good music. If there's too little tension, you'll fall flat; if there's too much tension, you'll be sharp." Our tension was too much, the music of our lives making a series of sharp chords, straining our ears. Jake and I wanted to resolve our conflict consistently, but the problem was that we weren't addressing the underlying issues. A cycle of arguing about a menial issue, silence and "I'm sorry" ensued.

Our love for ourselves and each other had to transform once we crossed the threshold between dating and marriage. I recall Jake gently saying, "Justina, the quiet doesn't fill me up like it fills you. I can't stay in the house all day. I need adventure." It was one of the first times Jake spoke up for himself, and we both realized we were doing everything we could to get only my needs met—*What will help Justina get out of pain? What will help Justina be okay? What will make Justina happy?* It was there we began the journey of understanding that only the Holy Spirit and I could answer these questions, just like only Jake and the Holy Spirit could answer the same questions for him.

Our rights as man and wife are to join in with the great chorus of each other's lives, to listen when a note is out of tune and give feedback, to cheer on and enjoy, not to control, resolve or re-create. We now know to stop and check our *own* needs for connection, rest, adventure and space when conflict arises. It is amazing what can happen when the Holy Spirit is invited in to untangle tension. Just recently, we found ourselves in an unexplainable series of disagreements where there was very little joy. We prayed together and asked the Holy Spirit to help us see what was going on. Neither of us really felt or heard anything. The following day, one of my friends at work began asking me questions about a trip I had taken the previous weekend. As I responded, I began to realize how difficult the trip was for me; I had brushed my feelings aside because of the fast-paced situation. As I answered her questions, I found myself crying because of what I had experienced. The unexpected but necessary moment opened up space for me to get honest with myself and the Father, which in turn, filled a deep need I had to process and let go of disappointment from the trip. That evening after work, I had the opportunity to communicate to Jake what truly been going on in my heart. I owned places where I projected my situation onto him. It felt so freeing to know that the Father heard us when we asked Him to help us in the midst of our disagreements, and *He* orchestrated the following day to bring resolve and closure. God wants to fight for our hearts and our marriages more than we can comprehend! When we give the Father an inch, He will rush in with a solution and help beyond what we can ask or imagine.

Prompt: Create a list of your needs and invite the Holy Spirit to look at the list with you. Where has He invited you to work through these needs with Him and where has He put people in your life to help you work through your needs together? Pray and invite the Holy Spirit to give you the courage to be honest about what you need.

two become one

Newlywed Series on Establishing Like-Minded Values in Marriage

Photography ———— Sydnee Mela & Morgan Campbell

The transition from being single to becoming united in covenant comes with unexpected struggles and joys. Conflicting habits and old patterns necessitate purposeful conversations between spouses to get on the same page; this way, new belief systems can be intentionally created with love, understanding and the Lord's perspective. Hear from two couples in our Cageless Birds community about the way they navigated creating new values in the beginning of their marriages. May the Holy Spirit use their testimonies to bring help and healing in your own marriage.

ON SPENDING TIME

from her ———— Lindsay Vance

For most of my young adult life I felt like I was competing against time. I had unrealistic expectations as to what could be accomplished in a day, and when I failed to meet these expectations, I blamed time. Before I was even finished with a project, I would compound my responsibilities and take on others, disregarding the consequences of my frenzied, tired heart. I elevated myself with busyness and thrived on the adrenaline I felt when I achieved a task. Marriage was the abrupt and beautiful storm that helped me unfurl my time-clenched fists. While neither Zac nor I came into marriage as experts in time management, his way of relating to time helped reveal to me the needy places in my heart. I was longing to slow down and direct my energy from a place of rest. For years I viewed time as prohibitive, unfavorable and sharp. I misunderstood its purpose, and this created distance between me and the Father. Through my marriage, God gave me permission to rethink my value for and expectations of time. He invited me to see that time is a gift—a boundary woven into the fabric of humanity, given as a way to measure the beauty that marks our lives.

In the early months of marriage, I commonly overwhelmed our weekends with robust to-do lists. On Sunday nights Zac and I felt disconnected, irritable and no more rested than at the end of our work week. My tendency to urgently spend time was hindering our joy and intimacy. Zac patiently and persistently

helped me see a better way. Now, when I propose we do four things on a Saturday, Zac counters that we shoot for two. We recognize that accomplishing two things from a place of rest is more nourishing than achieving many things from a mindset of scarcity. I am practicing in everyday moments how to operate from the belief that *how* I am while I'm doing something is just as important as *what* I do.

Since this belief system has taken root in my heart, I choose to spend my time based more on what is best for our hearts and less on what I think is expected of us. I am motivated to take Zac's needs into consideration when planning into our lives, knowing that his way of connecting to God, to others and to me is so different from what I need. In the same way that God uses time as a gift to show us love, I get to extend the generous gift of time to my husband. For example, Zac loves being outdoors. When he wants to spend time mountain biking, I get to encourage his adventure-driven alone time instead of reacting to the fear that we will miss out on time together. I become a partner in my husband feeling powerful and connected to God through nature. Time is a tool, enabling me to communicate love to Zac. We practice asking our hearts what we need and presenting these needs to the other with open-handedness and sincerity. Time slips its hand into ours and helps us meet these needs. It is a gift that turns a limited life of minutes into a love that is beyond measure.

from him ———— Zac Vance

I entered into marriage following two long seasons of higher education focused on dentistry. Surrounded by deadlines and exams at school, it was wise and necessary to let my course load dictate how I spent my time. I worked hard to make good grades and become a confident dentist. When I wasn't studying, I used my time passively, feeling deserving of a break from all my schooling. I spent hours watching a TV series or climbing at the gym—things that felt low stakes and served as an interruption to the intensity of dental school. The way I approached time management was adequate in the narrow lens of academia, but it didn't equip me to spend my time responsibly or thoughtfully in all areas of my life.

In theory, I knew marriage would be hard work. I had nearly a decade's experience of being a hard-working student, but this didn't translate to the hard work of connection that makes a marriage thrive. In our young marriage, there weren't any deadlines, and no one was grading me for my successes. My wife wasn't a professor demanding that I perform well and make

the "A", although sometimes I approached her like that. I was willing to pour in, but I didn't know how to stop checking out. I wanted her to tell me how to achieve being a good husband, so I could feel accomplished and then enjoy my deserved break. Lindsay didn't want a formulaic approach to marriage that could be outlined in a syllabus; she desired deep connection that's nurtured through vulnerable relationship.

Lindsay challenged me to see that every decision I made in regard to our time management had the ability to build or deteriorate our marriage. I couldn't just check off the connection box on a to-do list. I was responsible to stay connected to God and my wife in all things, even while I was meeting my needs in a personal way, like riding my bike or reading. I found that when I nurtured Lindsay's need for connection, she in turn helped nurture my own needs. She encouraged me to do the things I loved, but to do so thoughtfully, not as a way of coping and detaching. Time management is a tool that enables connection, and stewarded well, has the power to transform our marriage.

ON FORGIVENESS

from her ———— Jessie Miller

Before I was married, I always dreamed of being a gracious and compassionate wife, ready to mend moments of hurt with a heart full of forgiveness. I felt comfortable with this area in relationships. When things felt tense, I tried to fix them as soon as possible, whether that meant asking for or extending forgiveness. I believed that in marriage, it would only be easier for me to forgive because I would love my husband so much.

To my surprise when Chris and I got married I kept finding myself in moments where I could not seem to deliver. If we were in the car running late for a dinner with my parents, my mind would yell, "It's his fault! He could've moved faster! He should've made sure we left on time!" Even if we talked through it, prayed and he apologized for places he could have helped more, it just wasn't enough. This desire to punish before extending forgiveness felt like a dam, holding back the grace I wished I could extend. It hadn't felt like this with others, and I was struggling to see why this desire to punish was so strong with my husband, whom I loved so much. The Lord showed me that forgiving others had been "easy" for me, not because I was actually good at it, but because I was comfortable with taking the blame. In my view of forgiveness, someone had to be punished, and that someone was me. When things happened with friends, I could easily "forgive" them because I could find a way to see how it was actually my fault, not theirs. When I was single and running late, I always punished myself. I wanted to yell at Chris just like I had been yelling at myself for years. As we became one, my unwillingness to forgive and extend grace to myself was perpetuating an inability to forgive Chris. You can't fake it in marriage.

I have begun to practice self-compassion so that when I want to forgive Chris, I actually can. What Jesus endured on the Cross was punishment enough for every act that requires forgiveness. I do not need to make myself pay for what He already bought and offers me freely. Chris has partnered with me in this process of self-compassion. In a moment of friction, Chris will often stop me and discerningly ask, "Babe, what's really going on?" He's aware that how I'm feeling about myself affects how I feel about him and others. Only when I allow myself to receive the Father's grace can I truly give grace to Chris. Learning how to forgive myself has broken the dam, allowing me to forgive my spouse with a sincere heart. True, authentic forgiveness starts with self-compassion.

from him ———— Chris Miller

In our first year of marriage, I became increasingly aware of my misconceptions about forgiveness. I believed in the idea of it, but still found myself needing the other person to feel the punishment of space and silence. My tendency was to distance myself emotionally in a moment of conflict rather than to actually find resolve through courage and forgiveness. I learned from a young age that punishment was a normal way of moving on. Someone had to pay for the pain I felt.

This played out multiple times in our first year of marriage during moments of tension and conflict. If I felt attacked, or if my wife Jessie said something that offended me, I would shake my head with exaggerated disdain and walk silently into a different room or out of the house, symbolically shutting the door behind me. She would have to come and find me, proving that she felt the regret of our interaction, before I would forgive her. On the other side of the door, I began to feel the pain of disconnection and the lingering pride in my soul. The mirror of these moments made it unmistakably clear that I was not as holy as I would have liked to believe, and if intimacy and connection were the goal in our greatest moments of tension, my methods needed a major upgrade.

As we continued to learn each other, Jessie began to bravely open up about these moments, asking me if I was aware of my tendency to leave during moments of tension. She was vulnerable with how it affected her, what it communicated and what she desired in the future. It was the truth that I needed to hear, and the trust we were building created a solid foundation for practice.

In every corner of my life, the Lord has been showing me that punishment and shaming are not an effective response to places where I feel hurt or misunderstood. I used space and silence to communicate pain without courage, instead of taking the time to recenter and reconnect. With the help of the Holy Spirit, forgiveness looks like humbly and honestly owning up to my role, my behavior, and my communication in a moment. It looks like a true and honest apology that isn't withholding or vague. It's the honesty of saying *I was wrong and I am sorry* without employing blame. It's the vulnerability of asking *Would you be willing to forgive me?* without entitlement or control.

In marriage, as in life, forgiveness is crucial to staying intimately connected. In disagreements when I want to run, Jessie will patiently remind me of the power in vulnerability. She points me back to the Father and encourages me to not punish, but pursue reconnection. We are letting go of punishment as a prerequisite for forgiveness and embracing the vulnerability of staying present through tension—whether great or small.

BY LETTING GO OF PUNISHMENT AS A PREREQUISITE FOR
FORGIVENESS, WE ARE ABLE TO EMBRACE VULNERABLE HEARTS
CAPABLE OF ENGAGING A LOVE THAT STAYS CONNECTED.

ENVISION

Recipe for Casting Vision in Marriage ——— Justina Stevens

"Write the vision; make it plain on tablets, so he may run who reads it. For still the vision awaits its appointed time; it hastens to the end—it will not lie. If it seems slow, wait for it; it will surely come; it will not delay" (Habakkuk 2:2–3, ESV).

Marriage is an amazing, powerful gift. The beauty and adventure that takes place inside the mystery of two lives becoming one is nothing short of miraculous. A month before I said, "I do" to my husband, Jake, our mentors gave us an assignment to write a vision statement for our family. We were asked to take the time to articulate why we, the Stevens, were special. Why our legacy mattered and what we were going to do in our lifetime together.

Taking time with your spouse to search your hearts and the heart of the Father for your legacy puts you in a position of saying *I matter. We matter. Our family matters.* It gives the Father space to speak value over your marriage. It gives Him permission to come in and do what only He can do. It opens up the opportunity for us to give ourselves permission to work toward a goal. Ultimately, when we cultivate vision for our marriage we are walking out our identity as sons and daughters of God. Our calling on this earth is to do impossible things, and what is more impossible than transforming a family line—ending patterns of addiction, fear and shame, and raising children whose floor is our ceiling?

The key to writing a successful vision statement is to let yourselves get caught up in the miraculous reality that each of you and your family lines were handpicked by the Father to walk out something that no one else before you could. Marriage is the ultimate invitation to transformation, and transforming a family line is no small feat. It is a weighty goal and it requires intentionality and commitment to where you are headed. Two people in a marriage have the power to shift the direction of their family lines together, and in order to do that they have to approach their marriage with a reverent humility and dependence on the Lord to to see it through. In Proverbs it says, "Where there is no vision, the people perish…" (Proverbs 29:18, KJV). The feelings of love—butterflies, romance, thinking about each other all day—these things come and go with seasons, but identity and belonging are things that remain: through triumph and failure, arguments and laughter. It is vital for us to make the connection that the presence of vision is the presence of the Father, Son and Holy Spirit—where they are, vision follows. Without them, without vision, we are aimless and our lives lack purpose. The reality is that humanity without purpose is left to perish—and it is the Father's heart that we would not perish, but have everlasting life (John 3:16).

When Jake and I approached writing a vision statement it was challenging. Culture consistently told us that we were young, that life was too short to take things so seriously and that in the end, marriage was too hard after the newlywed feelings dissipated. It was easy to listen to these voices and avoid such serious conversations. After all, why put so much pressure on such a young couple, right? Wrong. In Western culture, our biggest enemy is apathy and not taking things seriously. When I say seriously, I don't mean solemn. Intentionality and purpose doesn't have to be a solemn process, but there is a part of the mystery of living a God-centered life that requires reverence—learning to engage the holiness of God in your normal, mundane life. As Jake and I began to process what we wanted to see change in our family, what we wanted to leave behind and pick up in our legacy, we were filled with so much courage. It filled us with the seriousness and the joy of pioneering something brand new. Committing to writing a vision statement actually made space in our hearts for change, and it empowered us to purge every fearful and skeptical opinion.

I want to charge you, the reader, to try something new. It's never too early and never too late to make a plan in your marriage. It's okay if your first vision statement is simple. Mine and Jake's was simple when we first did it and it has slowly grown over the years as we've weathered a few storms, grown in joy and expanded our family. You have what it takes to cultivate intentional, clear vision for your life together.

Prompt: Sit down with your spouse/fiancé and intentionally craft a vision statement for your family. Start by inviting the Holy Spirit to help you brainstorm a list of your common values, answering these questions:

1. *What kind of relationship do we want to have with one another?*
2. *How do we want to treat one another and speak to one another?*
3. *What kind of feeling do we want to have in our home?*
4. *What is the purpose of our marriage?*
5. *What do we want to be remembered by?*

Using your answers to the questions above, start crafting powerful statements about who you want to become. Take your time, and remember that this is your relationship, your life and your legacy. Make a point to use confident language: "We will" and "We will become" statements instead of phrases like "We hope we can…" This may take several drafts—ours did! Don't be afraid to edit and rewrite as you discover your vision as a family. Let joy be your compass as you craft this vision statement. Keep at it, and when you feel like you've landed, joyfully declare it over your lives together.

The Stevens' Vision Statement:

We, the Stevens, will be people that trust God: our Father, our Friend and Leader. We will choose each other, even when it takes time, remembering the honor of holding each other's hearts. We will be quick to repent and quick to forgive. We will be generous with what God has given us and fight for people around us, with love and joy as our compass. We will raise confident children who know they are loved. We will not hesitate to reach out for help when we need it. We will end every day looking into each other's eyes, assuming the best.

Values that
Transcend
Circumstance

An Interview on Establishing Values with Jonathan & Melissa Helser

By Allie Sampson & Erin Gravitt / Photography from Personal Collection

A short trip through the woods and we're at the strong wooden door of a familiar home. We have both been changed here—countless parties full of laughter, community nights alive with testimony and deep heart talks rich with repentance. To say that Jonathan and Melissa have impacted us is only scratching the surface; they have rerouted our path and helped guide us back to the Father over and over again. Their loving smiles and warm eye contact greet us at the door, and we're in it again—ready to hear the hearts of the leaders who have changed us.

Jonathan and Melissa Helser, fearless leaders and founders of the Cageless Birds, have been married almost two decades and have two amazing teenagers, Cadence and Haven. They've given their lives to see a generation transformed by the love of God through their worship worldwide and their discipleship schools and retreats at A Place for the Heart. Over the years they have given from the overflow of their intimacy with the Lord and one another to empower couples to thrive in covenant. In the inspiring comfort of their home in the North Carolina woods, we got to hear the stories that shaped their high honor for the Holy Spirit-given values that lead their family. Here they share honest testimonies of the power of overcoming and trusting the Lord in mountain highs, valley lows and everywhere in between. May their orchard of fruit of the Spirit champion you in your everyday to value His abiding presence above all.

COULD YOU NAME A FEW TOP CORE VALUES IN YOUR MARRIAGE RIGHT NOW?

JONATHAN: We have a value of serving one another. On the outside of my wedding ring, an old jeweler carved, "In serving one another we become free." Right before I got married, I learned that this phrase was what King Arthur had written on the round table where his leadership council of knights gathered. King Arthur's vision was for his kingdom to be built on the value of servanthood. I wanted to approach family the same way. I knew from the beginning that I wanted to serve my wife and my kids. It was actually one of the things I was most looking forward to, especially in parenting. I couldn't wait to change diapers...I know that sounds crazy, but I knew I would only have maybe three years to change diapers; I knew it was going to liberate something in my heart from my own selfishness and would give me time to speak into their lives like never before. I got to join God in the story

of their lives through my prayers. It's a joy to get to serve one another.

MELISSA: I think another core value we have is gratitude. When I read Scripture, I am overcome by how much Jesus thanked His Father. Jesus modeled gratitude that was so revolutionary—this awareness that there was always something to be thankful for before anything happened. I love the moment at Lazarus' tomb; everyone is so sad and angry, but Jesus is addressing the Father as if no one is there. He says, "I thank you Father that you hear me; you always hear me" (see John 11). He models this profound awareness and a posture of gratitude for things to come and for what has already happened. When I think about the people I want to be around the most, it's thankful people. About seven years ago we took a day trip to the mountains with a friend. It was the longest he had ever hung out with us, and he said, "Man, you guys say 'thank you' all day long—constantly under your breath. You take deep breaths and thank the Lord." We were completely unaware, but we did do that! I look back on that as one of the greatest compliments we have ever received. Even when I didn't know I was doing it, someone else was there to observe that we had cultivated something so beautiful in the secret. It blessed us both. It was a moment of being able to step back from our garden and say, "Our garden is flourishing."

IN YOUR ALMOST TWO DECADES OF MARRIAGE, WHAT'S BEEN THE IMPORTANCE FOR YOU TO HAVE A MARRIAGE BASED ON VALUES OVER RULES?

MELISSA: We married shortly after my twentieth birthday. Getting married really young and both of us coming from ministry families, we wanted so desperately to please and perform for the Lord and each other. The gift of getting married young was that, as much as we wanted to perform, we really wanted the better way. We knew there was a better way to do marriage and parenting. At twenty-two years old we had a baby—it was so counter-cultural. It created a tremendous neediness in our early twenties that propelled us into a value-driven pursuit. We've articulated that language more and more now, but back then it was a sacred pursuit we were on.

In our first year of marriage my disease came back really strong. The dynamic of suffering was so present in our early twenties—brand new marriage, new baby, and then you throw in the dynamic of disease, pain and suffering. That season confronted my tendency to perform. I thought, *I must be doing something wrong. If I fast, pray, read enough Scripture, do all these things, I should be healed.* It was really crushing, and I felt like I wasn't doing enough to get my healing, like it was never going to happen. I opened up to a friend about it, "I'm hitting a wall. I don't know what's happening. I can't get out of this rut. I feel overwhelmed with sadness that I can't make this thing happen." He looked in my eyes and asked me, "Melissa, is this season of your life producing good fruit?" He started listing the fruits of the Spirit, "Is it producing love? Gentleness? Self-control? Is this tension in your life producing good fruit?" I look back at that moment as the turning point of my twenties. I realized that if that season of suffering was producing good fruit, then that's exactly where I needed to be. It was an epiphany. He said, "They are going to know you by your fruit" (Matthew 7:16). Every religious voice, that Old Covenant voice that says, "Do better, try harder" lost its power. I thought, *Wow, I am becoming a powerful person in this season, in the middle of pain. I'm giving in to the presence of Jesus and the transforming work of the Gospel. This season is changing me.* That's where the shift of values happened for us, no more fear-driven choices, only joy would lead us from then on. The fruit of the Spirit is values-driven. Jesus gives so much value to seasons of grief in the Sermon on the Mount (see Matthew 5-7): "...Blessed are you when you mourn. Blessed are the merciful..." Suffering initiated that total perception shift for me to mature beyond rule-keeping. I'm still wrestling with this disease, but my inner world is so rooted and grounded in the heart of Jesus.

JONATHAN: When I think of rules versus values, it's like the Old Covenant versus the New Covenant. The Old Covenant is a list of "I have to do this," and the New Covenant is "I get to do this." Jesus took all of the law, rules and old prophets and put them into a value of love. If you cultivate love for yourself, love for the Lord and love for people, all the rules take care of themselves. The gravity of those values have held Melissa and I together many times. Our value for God's presence in our home has helped in moments where the fight would've lasted a little longer. The more we argue, the more we feel His presence leaving. Because we're aware of His presence, we feel the conviction to recognize when we need to humble our hearts and invite Him back to help us. That's translated to our kids, as well. For example, Cadence was watching a show at his friend's house and started to feel peace leave the room. When this happened he told his friend, "We can't watch this show. Let's turn it off." Our kids had boundaries on what they could and could not watch, however we couldn't monitor everything they saw. It was more valuable to teach them sensitivity to the Holy Spirit's presence.

MELISSA: When Cadence was around four years old, I prayed that God would give us wisdom in parenting him. God said, "Teach Cadence to need my Spirit. He will outgrow his need for you, but he'll never outgrow his need for me. Start now." That's a value system, being needy for Jesus, the Father and the Holy Spirit. Our kids will take that into every moment of their lives. Rules are very circumstantial, but values will transcend every circumstance. Whether that's in marriage or parenting, values are one of the most anchoring things we've cultivated and sought after.

WHAT DOES IT LOOK LIKE TO CHAMPION EACH OTHER IN MARRIAGE?

MELISSA: Championing means that I reach beyond myself to aid in the flourishing of another person. It's a posture of selflessness. Jonathan and I have an unusual set-up; we've worked together for eighteen years—there've been very few weeks we've been apart. We've learned how to do that well without it crushing us. You can't be champions in your personal life without also being champions in ministry and in your calling; you can't separate them. They are equally significant. Something we say a lot is "Encouragement is the table where community feasts." I really believe that for marriage, too. Being able to sow in and see beyond where we are to the greater person that we are becoming, it takes living in the Spirit. I don't think that's reduced to coaches or strong leaders. It's a quality, trait, value system for every believer. Every believer has the ability to see beyond where someone is and see where they're heading.

We realized very early on that our ideal versions of life were very different from one another. The golden thread that pulled us together was our genuine, pure love for the Kingdom of Heaven to come to Earth. We both bring a specific part of Heaven to Earth, and we've actually had to learn how to champion that in one another. I never would have started writing music if

I didn't marry Jonathan—learning to write in solitude, the secret place and practicing getting still before the Lord. That's essential to the human soul; now I know that. People were my life—ministry, pastoring. Jonathan certainly wouldn't be leading a community if he hadn't married me. We love what each other loves without becoming that other person. We enter into each other's worlds. Where he can go into the woods and sing and process before the Lord in song for hours and hours, that's not my go-to way of spending my time. And where I can spend hours and hours in counseling sessions and meeting with people—that would completely drain Jonathan. We've had to learn this beautiful giving-in without abandoning who we are. I'm loving this season because we're confidently pursuing giving one another space to be who we are without needing to be the same. I am a champion of his solitude. Jonathan is a champion of my love for pastoring and coaching. The way we weave in and out of that storyline without having to do it together all the time has been huge.

JONATHAN: When we first got married, we didn't play music together. Then, about ten years ago, when Melissa's joints started having a lot of breakthrough because of the medicine she was on, I got her a 1979 Guild guitar. The doctors told her she'd never be able to play the guitar, but the night I gave her the guitar she wrote *Explode My Soul*. When husbands and wives see desires in one another and do everything they can to make those things come to pass, those simple things are championing one another. Now we're making music together—recording albums, traveling, touring— it's amazing and there's a lot of tension in it. But no one's encouragement means more to me than Melissa's. There are moments when we look at each other across the stage and I am so delighted. I'm watching Melissa do what she's made to do, and I'm standing behind her; I do what I do, because she is there beside me. We are tag-teaming, in each other's corners, fighting for one another. We are always fighting for each other's hearts.

WHAT HAS GOD TAUGHT YOU ABOUT COMPASSION IN THE REALM OF FAILING AND FORGIVING?

MELISSA: Jonathan says, "Without tension you can't make music." As musicians we know that's true. In the natural, if you take the tension out of the guitar, it can't make music; no sound comes from it. Too much tension,

and everything will pop and break and you'll hurt each other. An appropriate amount of tension creates music. Looking back at getting married young, having kids and the disease, there was so much tension. But when tension is submitted to the Lord, there's a song that comes out of your life, there's a capacity to deal with it. Tension and failing is a part of life. Learning to forgive is something that every human soul has to learn in order to thrive. Learning how to forgive is a life essential whether you are married or not. Don't believe the lie, "If we were a good Christian couple we would never fight." That lie is a robbery of what marriage can actually produce. Tension produces intimacy and connection when it is submitted to the Lord.

When you see mistakes as an invitation to be kind to yourself, you'll start to realize, *The more that I give in to humility personally, the deeper my well gets.* When you practice that, you'll have so much more to give to your best friend, your spouse and kids. That's the greatest key I can give anyone: Practice, practice, practice. Always give yourself permission to practice.

> Don't believe the lie, "If we were a good Christian couple we would never fight." That lie is a robbery of what marriage can actually produce. **Tension produces intimacy and connection** when it is submitted to the Lord.

BECOMING AN ALLY

Recipe for Balance in Processing with Your Spouse ——— Jessie Miller

Photograph ——— Sydnee Mela & Morgan Campbell

Man, I can't believe he did that again today. Why won't he just give in? I was exhausted after another full day at work and couldn't stop thinking about the standoff I'd had with a student that morning. As I got in the car, tears filled my eyes. *Papa, help me understand why he's still so disrespectful. I'm trying so hard to help him.* Frustration was a recurring theme at work. Many of my workdays ended with me feeling depleted, discouraged and in need of space to process. As I pulled out of the parking lot, deep breaths of *Help me, Holy Spirit* filled my lungs. I was aware of my need to be understood and supported, and previous cycles of handling disheartening moments had taught me to take my frustrations to the Lord before taking them home to my husband, Chris.

I hadn't always known how to handle this need. In the early days of teaching, I felt so overwhelmed sometimes that I'd come home and spill it all, replaying the entire moment for Chris at full emotion. Someone needed to know *exactly* how I *really* felt about what was going on. I still felt limited by my own passivity at work and felt liberated when I could finally vent to Chris and say what I really wanted to say in the heat of the moment. Everything that had been bottled up was finally out and I felt like myself again. However, the full-of-energy husband I'd come home to was now exhausted, worn out by the intensity of my situation and the pressure I'd put on him to have an answer...or at least feel my pain. I was lighter, but the weight of my problem was now on Chris' shoulders. He was no longer a partner to share with, but a target for my unreleased frustration.

On the days when I saw Chris through this filter, every interaction was fueled by the impulse to get my needs met. I expected him to consistently check in, pick up on my hints that I was struggling and make me feel better. Simple phone calls turned into sources of tension. On a tough day, I would call Chris and ask him how he was doing with the real goal of getting him to ask *me* how *my* day was. If he didn't, I'd get mad and start criticizing him in my mind. *That doesn't sound that bad. My day was way harder than that. Why won't you just ask me about mine?* Chris saw through my tactics and would avoid asking me about my day. I could feel his resistance. Entitlement set in as we fought indignantly for our needs: him needing to connect without my emotional monologues and me needing to process and unwind. Our conversations were marked by entitlement and comparison. We listened while keeping tally marks of whose day held tougher ground to plow.

The reality is, I have a very pastoral and caring husband. In the early days of our marriage, he would let me dump my frustrations on him as a way for me to feel cared for. He genuinely wanted to support me, and I genuinely wanted to share. In the end, what we were missing was balance. We desperately needed to learn how to process in a healthy way and draw boundaries. Chris couldn't change my problems at work, just like I couldn't change his. For the sake of our connection, our romance and our enjoyment of spending time together, we needed to make some changes.

We began asking each other and the Lord for some keys to help us actually connect in those moments. We love communication and sharing with one another. It wasn't that Chris wasn't interested in what was happening at school, but I realized replaying entire scenarios at full emotion didn't allow room for Chris to enter into a conversation with me. At the end of my monologues, there would be nothing left

for him to say. He couldn't possibly match the emotion of what I had communicated. I began to engage the truth that, because the Lord was with me in the classroom, He was the one that could help me fully unpack those difficult moments. He knew firsthand how tough it had been. He was there with me and could bear the weight of what I had experienced. I'd give Him all of my emotion and let Him fill me with His peace. I would still share with Chris, but I was no longer placing all of my unresolved emotion at his feet. This left room for my husband to come in as an ally. He was a valuable contributor to my process instead of a voiceless target for my frustration.

Chris and I also began drawing boundaries around how much we processed work with each other. We noticed that it wasn't working for all of our quality time to be spent over-processing the same types of scenarios. We asked the Lord for ideas and began intentionally carving out time to do things that weren't work-related. We went to concerts, saw movies and hung out with couples who were doing completely different things from us. Taking a step back from our daily grind and making powerful choices about how we wanted to spend our time gave us vision for our connection.

The greatest gift that came from this season was the understanding that Chris was not just a place to vent, and I was not a victim who needed to be rescued. We were and are a team. He was an ally in my beautiful mission to see the Kingdom come in my classroom. Our bond held the truths that I was valuable, capable of powerful, love-based leadership and had full access to the Holy Spirit. As spouses, we get the chance to act as an advocate to help remind the other of their worth and capability while encouraging them to be brave and move forward from these truths. Chris and I have learned that our processing is only as meaningful as our follow-through with the people we encounter at work. We are there to help empower, not cast judgment, vilify, take offense or connect with negativity. Because we let each other in, we have a storehouse of shared stories. Victories and failures, mistakes and discoveries, heartaches and breakthroughs all rest safely within our connection.

When I look back on what Chris and I learned in that season, I love what I see. Countless moments like the ones I had in the car, taking deep breaths and making space for the Lord to speak. He always met me in the emotion. Unraveling the tangled places, offering compassion and assurance, "Jessie, you're right. These moments are really hard. Keep pressing in. You are so capable and your kindness is making a difference." These conversations with Him empowered me to walk through the front door of my house more rested and full of peace. When I look over my season of teaching with the Trinity, I cherish the feeling of a steady hand holding mine, looking out over the harvest with me. My ally, my confidant, my husband.

Prompt: Are you unleashing frustrations, entitlement or comparison on your spouse and expecting them to meet your emotional needs? Take an honest look at your heart and invite the Holy Spirit to give you practical ideas for boundaries in your processing. Make a list in your journal and invite your spouse to do the same. Together, pick a boundary to implement that you both feel joy on. In a week, talk through how it went together. Are you experiencing more joy, more excitement, more connection? If so, keep going! If not, ask the Lord for a new idea. Enjoy exploring what would benefit your marriage together.

Overflow

Recipe for Living from Overflow ———— *Jonathan David Helser*

Photography ———— *Polaroids from Paris, France*

One of my kids' favorite things in life is what they have affectionately titled a "Daddy Date." A Daddy Date is exactly what the title suggests—a special date with just their dad. What makes this so significant is that there is no one else allowed on a Daddy Date; it's just one of them and me. Whatever adventure we go on—from seeing a movie to getting ice cream or going to the park—the one thing they can always expect on these dates is that they have their father all to themselves.

Recently, while I was on one of these dates with my son, I started thinking about when Adam had God all to himself in Eden. We don't know how long that moment lasted before Eve entered the story, but I like to imagine it was an extended time of friendship between a Father and His son. I believe they shared many long walks, the Father showing off His creation to His son. Days were filled with delight and

joy unspeakable as they discovered one another in a world without sin and shame. There was even a wild date to the zoo when God brought all the animals of the earth to Adam, for His son to name each one.

After these sacred moments of a Father and son enjoying one another's company, the story shifts as God places Adam in a deep sleep and pulls a rib from his side. From this rib God fashions a woman. Now, we see another date begin between the Father and His first daughter. We don't know how long this moment lasted either, but remember we are talking about a God to whom one day is like a thousand years. I imagine Adam passed out in a deep sleep in the corner of Eden, while the Father takes His daughter all over creation showing off His handiwork. Just as Adam had his own time alone with God, Eve shared her own moment with the Father before she met her husband. I personally think that God savored this moment and stretched it out as long as possible. God had to know that once Adam saw Eve, Adam would be so head over heels in love with her that it might be a while before God could have a date like this again.

The scene shifts again when God "brought her unto the man" (Genesis 2:22, ASV). Just like weddings have replayed ever since, the Father walks His daughter down the aisle of Eden to meet her groom and lifelong companion. Adam awakes from his deep sleep to see the desire of his heart coming toward him. Both Adam and Eve have had their hearts filled up in relationship with God, and they begin their marriage loving one another from that overflow. In this first marriage we see God's design and dream. Marriage is not two broken halves becoming one. Marriage is two whole hearts becoming one. In this detail of the creation story is hidden one of the greatest keys for marriage and relationship. We are designed to love one another from the overflow of our relationship with God. True relationship is not about what we can get from one another, but what we can give to one another.

A wise man once told Melissa and I in our marriage counseling, "You will never meet all of your spouse's emotional needs in marriage." I have to be honest that his statement sounded kind of crazy to both of us. We were in our early twenties and so madly in love with each other that we thought our young love could fix any problem. We were both politely nodding our heads as our mentor shared, but we were both thinking, *What in the world is marriage for then?* We had both assumed that in marriage all of our emotional needs would get met. Our mentor went on to unpack this truth: God's love is the only thing that can fill the deep places in the heart of every person. If we demand our marriage to meet our every need, we will be greatly disappointed. These words of wisdom have saved us many heartbreaks and have set us up for so much success in our relationship.

Recently I was having a rather rough day. It all came to a head while I was trying my best to be a "good" husband and get dinner ready for my family. I was getting frustrated at the smallest little thing and letting everyone know it through my very passive-aggressive huffs and puffs. It had been a very busy week and I hadn't taken much time to be alone and center my heart with the Father. Right in the middle of another round of huffs and puffs my beautiful bride gently placed her hand on my shoulder and said, "Babe, I think you need to go take a walk and spend some time with the Lord. I will finish up dinner. Just come back in twenty minutes." After eighteen years of marriage, I have learned to listen to this wise woman. I wasn't always so quick to listen, but over the years I've learned that God really knew what He was talking about when He said, "It's not good for man to be alone." My wife can see the blind spots I can't see about myself, and on this evening she was seeing right through my outer frustration into the deeper need my heart was crying out for. When I returned to the dinner table twenty minutes later, I was a different person. I was filled with the joy and love of the husband and father I was meant to be. I am so thankful that my wife knows me well enough to know when I am running on empty and need to be refilled by the Father.

Love began with a Father choosing us and daring to give everything to save us. He made the greatest sacrifice the world will ever know to prove His love to us. "We love Him, because He first loved us" (I John 4:19, NIV). The beautiful invitation in every relationship is to love others with this love He first gave. The words of Jesus so beautifully sum up this design of overflow: "A new command I give you: Love one another. As I have loved you, so you must love one another" (John 13:34, NIV).

Prompt: Set aside a block in your schedule this week for a date with your Father. Carve out a time when you can turn off all the distractions and just be with Him. Think of something that you will really enjoy doing with just Him. Don't let it be a stuffy, religious quiet time, but allow it to be a time filled with joy like Adam and Eve experienced in Eden. Maybe take a long hike or find a quiet place to watch Him paint a sunrise or sunset. Let His peace fill you where there is tension; let His joy kiss the places that have become dull. Pour out your heart to Him and let His presence refill your heart, so you may love others from the overflow of His love. Toward the end of your time with the Lord, take a few moments to pray out loud for the relationships in your life. I have found that when I cultivate time alone praying for my wife, my children and my friends, my love for them increases in incredible ways. As you re-engage your relationships pay attention to how this time with the Father affects the way you respond to your spouse, children and the people around you. Remember, you were made to love from overflow of His love.

seek to ———

UNDER

S T A N D

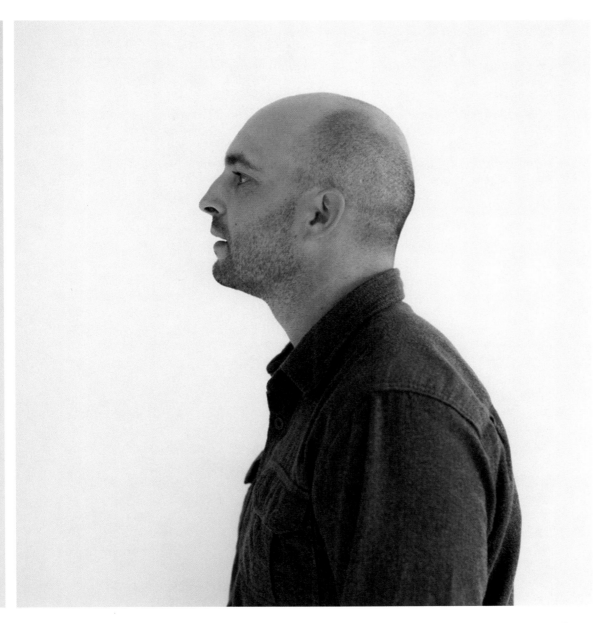

Recipe for Creating a New Normal in Marriage ———— Jason Vallotton

Photography ———— Sydnee Mela & Morgan Campbell

I remember the first time I went to visit my wife Lauren's family for Christmastime. We all came downstairs and were getting ready to open presents on Christmas morning. I noticed that everyone had their own notepad, and I wondered, *What's going on? Great, I'm the only one sitting here without a notepad.* As each gift was given, Lauren's family would read the card carefully and the name of the gift-giver and write it down, so they could send a thank you card. In Lauren's family culture, everyone has been taught that you send a thank you card for a gift. If you don't, then it's considered rude. Now, in my family's "normal" for Christmas, you don't even know who gave the gift; you're just tearing apart the wrapping paper and shaking the envelope to see if it has money in it. Our family's norm is just yelling out "thank you!" and moving on.

When Lauren and I started to do Christmases in our marriage, she realized right away that it's foreign to me to write thank you notes for everything. If I stayed the night over at her parents' home, I had to learn that a thank you note was expected of me. Their value system is: *You express your gratitude when others show you kindness.* I could really seem like a careless person if Lauren didn't fully understand where I came from. We spent a lot of time in the beginning of our marriage exploring our normals like this one, so that I don't judge her as ridiculous for always demanding our family to write thank you cards for every little thing, and she doesn't judge me as inconsiderate. Our kids don't write thank you notes, but we do sit down and call Grandma to verbally thank her for a gift. We've decided that this is a great bridge between having to send every single person a note and actually letting them know that you feel really thankful. The value is still being met in the new normal we've created for our own family.

There is a verse in the book of Proverbs that has been an inspiration for me in learning to understand other peoples' normal. Proverbs 18:2 (NIV) says, "Fools find no pleasure in understanding but delight in airing their own opinions." It is wisdom to look beyond our own understanding and develop value for someone else's. It's both humbling and enlightening. There are reasons people have their normals and what could seem silly to us can become valuable when understood.

Exploring norms in a marriage means that as a couple you both talk to each other. As Lauren and I get in various scenarios and we find something new or strange, we ask objectively, "Hmm, why do you do that? Explain that to me." Our family value system around doing that is: "We prioritize connection in our relationship." I have a value to know what she believes is normal and true, because somehow we're going to decide what is right for our family. The challenge in marriage is when our normal way of viewing things is so different than our spouse and vice versa, that we both get stuck in thinking that our normals are right and everything else is wrong. When you grow up in your family's normal for so long, you're taught that there is a right way to do something—in celebrating holidays, communicating, raising

kids. The truth is there are a lot of right ways. When your spouse has a different normal, it can be scary. We like safety and feeling comfortable. Plus, we have value systems built around our normals. It all goes south when couples lose the ability to adapt and look at situations objectively.

There are rules of engagement when it comes to handling conflict well in marriage. First and foremost, seek to understand. This is paramount. If Lauren seems agitated, I can say, "What's wrong with you?" in a million different ways. I can say, "Looks like something's wrong," in an annoyed and condescending tone. I can angrily raise my voice, "What's wrong with you!?" Or I can, with genuine inquiry, ask, "Hey Babe, is everything okay?" Our number one goal is: "Seek to understand." It doesn't matter if it's a giant thing or a small, petty thing. Anything can throw us off, so I'm going to seek to understand, and I'm going to listen.

A lot of people make peace their goal, which sounds really awesome in a relationship, but when we don't actually address issues we don't solve anything. Couples that make peace their goal are very passive and their relationship is very shallow. They end up living like roommates. Dialogue might sound like this:

Wife: I'm going to go get the kids.
Husband: Okay, sounds great.
Wife: Um, Katie's not doing great in high school.
Husband: Okay, do we have a solution for that?
Wife: Well, I think she's going to do some tutoring.
Husband: Alright. Great.

There aren't any deeper questions, like, "How do you feel about it?" There's no emotion expressed. Eventually, that marriage blows up because keeping the peace is full of self-protection instead of vulnerability, authenticity and courage. The enemy is not conflict. Lauren and I have conflict all the time, around the kids, around work—it's not bad. It's just a place for me to think, *Okay, right now what's important is that we are connected at the end of this.*

Conflict is something that has to happen in a marriage relationship. Our ability to navigate through conflict as spouses creates a beautiful trust between us. When we both know that we can be different and that our differences don't break us apart, conflict actually creates safe space for us to explore one another. Ultimately, conflict should be a place of strength.

Prompt: Pray and ask the Lord to grow your understanding of and connection with your spouse. Journal His response. If you're really trying to learn and are committed to growth in your marriage, then you need to take steps to help ensure it happens. Once you've heard the voice of the Lord, start taking practical steps to help you grow into who He is calling you to be. If your goal is to do conflict well this year, then you need to make a plan.

PLAN

make a ——

1. Ask the Holy Spirit for a phrase to help you transform in this season. For example, if you are hoping to be more understanding and kind toward your spouse, perhaps it would be *Slow down and seek to understand* to help you remember to stop assuming and start asking more questions.

2. Write yourself a daily reminder. On your mirror in your bedroom or bathroom, use a dry erase marker to write a one-sentence reminder to support your goal. Read it out loud to yourself every day.

3. If you have a smartphone, set midday and evening alarms to remind you of your phrase. These really quick reminders need to be read on a regular basis so that when you're in the heat of the battle, you'll remember it actually isn't a battle between you and your spouse—this is simple learning and growing. Read your reminders every single day—it makes a big difference!

4. Check in regularly. Ask yourself: *Am I growing in this? Am I following through?*

GET TING HON EST

A PRACTICAL TOOL *for* PROCESSING YOUR EMOTIONS

JONATHAN DAVID &
MELISSA HELSER

When I look back on my life, I want to know with assurance that I showed up the most for my marriage. I want to feel confident that I spent energy and time on that relationship more than anything else. I believe wholeheartedly it is one of the greatest gifts to the human soul: companionship. To have a friend, lover and comrade in this life journey is a gift beyond measure. Jonathan and I got married a month after my twentieth birthday. He was twenty-one and we were ready to take the world by storm. Even with all the passion of a young couple so deeply in love, we realized early on that it was going to require a tremendous amount of work, way more than we thought.

About six months into our first year of marriage the skin and bone disease I had been healed of two years prior came back with a vengeance. Nothing can prepare you for life's wildernesses. They come with no warning, and in a moment you are required to recalibrate to your new surroundings and find yourself and God in the middle of it all. The pressure that the sickness put on our marriage is difficult to describe.

LIFE IS PROFOUNDLY HARD.

This is where I pause and let the tears fall. I am not ashamed of the heartache and the wrestle that comes with it. Suffering has the potential to either crush us or uncover a strength beyond what we thought was possible.

We wrestled with God and His will. We cried, laughed, screamed, prayed over and over and decided to go on living. Our process wasn't perfect but what was formed in that season is still with us.

DEPENDENCY AND HONESTY.

I gladly talk about dependency and honesty over and over because these two pillars have saved me and saved our marriage. Learning to lean into the triune God with no hesitation, no shame. Shedding the layers of striving and proving that I could handle it and be the perfect "Christian": pray hard enough, have enough faith, fast, wait patiently on the Lord, don't waiver in your belief... This mounting pressure created distance between me and those around me. I couldn't soften with Jonathan until I learned to soften with the Lord and myself. I had to learn vulnerability. I believe we learn true vulnerability with others when we are brave enough to risk it with our own hearts. Risking feeling exactly what we feel, with no apologies. Giving ourselves permission to go the distance with our own hearts so that

we can in turn be open and honest with the ones we love. If I couldn't be honest with myself or the Lord, how would I ever be honest with Jonathan? I had no idea how to process my life with the Lord. When I would sit down to have "God Time," I felt overwhelmed and confused. "Just read your Bible...Just let it go and forgive...Just have faith... Just say you're sorry." These are the things I would tell myself over and over.

Without dependency and honesty, our human default is to go into behavioral management: just trying to be better without ever understanding what is really going on underneath the surface. Learning to process honestly before the Lord and acknowledge what is really going on has transformed every part of our lives. The greatest gift we can give to you, the reader, is our vulnerability with the Holy Spirit. We are so excited to give you a real tool and not just words on a page. This is a practical tool that is not meant to just fix you but transform the way you love yourself, God and others. We have given decades to empowering people in real life. We desire for you to grow beyond surviving to thriving.

In John 14:6 in the NIV translation, Jesus says, "I will ask the Father, and He will give you another advocate to help you and be with you forever, the Spirit of truth..." Here, Jesus promises the gift of the Holy Spirit. He promised to not leave us alone and wanted us to have a helper in our everyday life. He went beyond God with us to God in us. The Holy Spirit and the voice of the Lord take this tool beyond self-help to an invitation of the transforming presence of the Almighty into your everyday world.

In the next pages we are opening the book of our lives and giving you two everyday examples where we have hit conflict and decided not to stuff it and move on, but made the choice to practice vulnerability and honesty. We sat and took the time to practice the tool and navigate through our hearts with the Holy Spirit. Relationships are hard, and it is life-changing to learn how to fight for them the appropriate way. May you feel liberated and ready to give in to conflict and find the Lord there. This tool has not only transformed our hearts personally, but our whole community. It has given us real help in moments of confusion, conflict and feeling emotionally out of control. It has taught us the power of honesty and vulnerability with the Father, Son and Holy Spirit. We desire for you to find the freedom of recognizing that your heart is significant and what you're feeling matters. We use it all the time and consistently feel the fruit of valuing our process. May you receive the breakthrough we all long to have.

Oregon, 2012

THE HONESTY TOOL

1. STOP AND ASK

Pray, "Holy Spirit, I need your help. What is really going on?"

To stop and ask for help is to invite the Holy Spirit and His perspective. Inviting His presence into your process is one of the most powerful practices. He has every solution and is fully committed to you. He is the Spirit of Truth and is ready to empower your new process.

"Help me, Lord my God; save me according to your unfailing love" (Psalms 109:26, NIV).

2. GET HONEST

Get your journal and pen and go sit somewhere quiet. Take the risk to write your most honest prayer.

Include your thoughts, emotions and behavior in the situation. This action is humbly admitting that you need help from the One who knows you best. David consistently practiced brutal honesty and neediness for the Father throughout the Psalms. He had a confidence that God wasn't afraid of his humanity, which produced an intimacy that still ministers to our hearts today.

"Search me, God, and know my heart; test me and know my anxious thoughts" (Psalms 139:23-24, NIV).

3. REFLECT

After completing your most honest prayer, take a moment to read what you wrote and reflect.

Ask yourself, *Are these thoughts true? Am I believing any lies about myself, another person or God?* Underline and create a list of the thoughts and lies you want to exchange for the truth. We cannot give away what we do not own. Learning to own your honest beliefs is the beginning of transformation. It allows us to enter into an exchange with the Father where He replaces lies with truth.

"…we take captive every thought to make it obedient to Christ" (II Corinthians 10:5, NIV).

4. LISTEN & EXCHANGE

Pray, "Holy Spirit, speak to me the truth." Journal His response.

Give Him permission to speak into the vulnerable places in your heart. It is vital that you land this practice in the Father's voice. This tool isn't for self-help, it is meant to cultivate dependency on the Trinity. Always practice landing in His opinion. If the voice of the Lord created the heavens and the earth, He can recreate your inner world. This step requires faith and risk and is always worth it! An indicator that you are on the right track is if you feel seen by the Lord and His nature fills your heart—joy, compassion, peace, love.

"Then you will know the truth, and the truth will set you free" (John 8:32, NIV).

THE
LONDON
MELISSA'S
HONESTY TOOL
TRIP

Many years ago, Jonathan and I were chatting through our upcoming schedule. We had been gone for twenty-one days overseas and had just gotten home and settled. There was an event that was happening in England with some worship leaders we had been longing to connect with and I was so excited about going. When Jonathan sat down and asked, "Hey can we talk about England?" I said, "Sure," thinking he wanted to chat through details. He proceeded to say, "I am not sure it's a good idea for you to go." I was surprised at his tone and taken aback by his question. "What do you mean?" I said. "Well we just got back and I don't know if your body can handle another long trip. You're in so much pain, do you think it's wise?"

I sat there shocked and... let's just say I totally freaked out. It was one of those moments when a part of you is starting to fly off the rails and another part of you is saying, *Be calm, it's not what you think, don't overreact.* Learning to actually listen to the part of your heart that is saying *be calm* is an art I am still learning and that day was definitely not the day. I completely lost my cool and started saying things like, "You don't want me there, do you? I am too much of a burden, aren't I? You don't even like leading worship with me. It's just too much. I am too much." He was looking at me like, *What in the world is wrong with you?* "Melissa,

Asheville, NC 2018

that is not what I said." As I replied with, "That is exactly what you said!" I also might have been raising my voice, backing away. I eventually just went into my bedroom and slammed the door. I am not proud of that moment but what happened after that I am very proud of.

I stood in my room leaning against my door, panting and starting to cry. I had just been taught to ask the Holy Spirit for help. I took a deep breath and said out loud, "Holy Spirit, what is going on?" Immediately I felt the presence of the Holy Spirit. It was time to use the tools. I pulled out my journal and began to write. One of the main tools we were taught was to stop and ask for help and then identify if there are any lies we are believing in the moment that are fueling such strong reactions. I know it seems simple but it truly was revolutionary. Instead of just trying to figure it out on my own and punishing Jonathan with silence or passive-aggressive behavior until I felt better or he apologized over and over, I learned to take responsibility for my heart. *What am I feeling in this moment and why did I just react like that?* Getting intentional with our hearts takes time and a willingness to actually do the work. It isn't easy. We all want a quick fix but in relationships that doesn't exist. We have to be willing to do the work.

1. STOP AND ASK THE HOLY SPIRIT FOR HELP.
2. GET HONEST WITH HOW YOU'RE FEELING.
3. REFLECT. ARE THERE ANY LIES I AM BELIEVING?
4. LISTEN TO GOD'S VOICE AND EXCHANGE YOUR THINKING FOR HIS.

---

1. Holy Spirit, what's going on? why did I freak out when Jonathan asked if it's wise for me to go to England?

2. Father, I feel totally lost in this situation and need your help. Jonathan doesn't want me to go to England and I just flipped out. I feel so angry. I hate being sick. I'm so tired of it. I know Jonathan is, too. I feel like such a burden and it's so much easier to travel without me. I hate feeling incapable and weak. Am I always going to miss out because of this disease? I wanted to go so bad and I am disappointed. I am upset, angry, frustrated. This whole situation makes me feel alone. I hate it when I overreact. Is this season ever going to be over? I feel like you're never going to heal me.

3. I am a burden. Jonathan doesn't like traveling with me. The Lord is never going to heal me. I always overreact.

4. My beautiful Melissa. Take a deep breath. Your life is not a race and you are not in a hurry. I have been with you and am consistently with you. I will remove the fear of "missing it" and give you steadfast love. Look at me. I am right on schedule. You are not going to be sick forever. I am a Father of perfect timing. I am inviting you into deep trust. I give you in this moment the gift of trust. Trust Jonathan. He loves you and knows you and is my gift to you.

CLOSING THOUGHTS

Can you believe how beautiful the voice of the Lord is? Reading what He said years later, I feel His presence, His promise, His closeness. I know this seems so intense and honestly it was. My heart was hurting, and getting brutally honest with what was really there brought heartbreak and a total relief. In that moment, I had to recognize that I did make an agreement with a lie about God, Jonathan and myself and repent so that I can truly continue to believe the truth.

THE SHOWER DOOR

JONATHAN'S HONESTY TOOL

This tool has helped me so much. It's amazing to see how much growth there's been in my life since I began using it. It's helped me get in tune with what's actually going on in my heart; to not only identify my patterns but to understand what's at the root of my behavior. Learning to be honest with my heart and to get vulnerable before God has been one of the most impacting tools in my spiritual life as a man. Instead of staying in cycles of mistakes, repeating the same thing over and over and shaming myself for it, I am able to get clarity and make powerful choices to change. Here's one example of a time when I found myself caught in a pattern, and the honesty tool helped me process what was really happening:

When we built our house ten years ago, we added an unfinished basement. We had dreams to turn it into an apartment one day so we could host our friends and family who travel. Melissa and I travel a lot and we know how valuable it is to have somewhere peaceful to rest. About three years ago, we decided it was time to finish the basement. I had decided that when the time came to complete the apartment, I was going to

Sophia, 2000

have a perfect attitude toward Melissa. I had a passion to do the whole thing without any fights or arguments and to stay at peace the whole time. The renovation took weeks to complete and I'd done it! We were so close to finishing and we'd not gotten into a single argument! The only thing left was installing the shower door in the bathroom.

The shower was the big splurge on our basement— it was this beautiful slate tile shower in the bathroom, and we'd had to order a custom glass door for it. We'd been waiting for it to arrive when Melissa and I left for a ministry trip. The night we got home, there it was on our doorstep. I was so excited to finish the basement and decided to go downstairs right then and install it. "Babe, are you sure you want to do this tonight?" Melissa asked, "It's late and you're really tired." I said, "No, this is awesome! We're so close and I'm going to finish it. It'll be great, I'm going to go do it!"

So I went downstairs and everything was going great. I was taking my time and doing everything right. Long story short, I thought I'd cut the glass to the right size, but it ended up getting stuck and scratching this beautiful tile. As soon as the scratch happened, Melissa popped her head in the door and said, "How's it going, Babe?" And I just totally snapped at her, "Will you just leave and come back later?" I was so irritated. She seems to show up right when I make a mistake.

Before she walked in I realized the mistake I had made and said to myself, "Why am I so stupid?" As soon as I heard myself say that, I realized I was shaming myself, and knew I needed to stop and do some heart work. I put the shower door down and before I picked it up again the next day, I did the honesty tool.

1. STOP AND ASK THE HOLY SPIRIT FOR HELP.
2. GET HONEST WITH HOW YOU'RE FEELING.
3. REFLECT. ARE THERE ANY LIES I AM BELIEVING?
4. LISTEN TO GOD'S VOICE AND EXCHANGE YOUR THINKING FOR HIS.

---

1. Holy Spirit, what is going on? Will you help me understand why I snapped at Melissa and myself?

2. Father, I run to you instead of the voices of shame. I have tried so hard to do this construction project with a good attitude and I really blew it. I feel so stupid when I make mistakes. I am tired of shaming myself when I mess up. I am exhausted with this feeling of not being enough. When I make a mistake, I feel like I am all alone and it's all up to me to fix it. I am weary of trying so hard to be perfect. It feels like you demand perfection. Help me see that you are a Father that is full of grace and your goodness is always bigger than my mistake. It always seems like Melissa walks in the room right when I screw up. I don't want to react to Melissa with frustration when she sees my weakness.

3. I am stupid. I am alone. God demands perfection. I have to be perfect. Its all up to me to fix everything.

4. Jonathan David, I love you because of who you are, not based on what you do. I never said the thought that has controlled you: "It must be perfect." This yoke is not the way of sonship. You have allowed the accuser to place demands on your heart that I have not required of you. Come, my son, and rest in my unfailing love. Trust again in the wonder of my grace. My ways are not to embarrass you and shame you. I am the protector of your heart + soul. I have given you Melissa to help you. You don't have to perform for her. Perfection and performance have robbed you of true relationship. I am setting you free to enjoy abundant life. It's your privilege to make mistakes because it is my joy to work all things together for your good.

CLOSING THOUGHTS

This was a powerful moment for me. If I'd ignored what I was feeling instead of acknowledging it, I would have missed out on the truth and healing that the Holy Spirit was offering. As a man, I could easily live my whole life ignoring my feelings. It would be much easier for me to suppress the feeling of being stupid, to call it nothing and move on. The discipline of acknowledging and owning what I'm feeling has required a commitment to do the work. Just like any other discipline, it takes practice but there is also great payoff. I'm a better husband, a better father and a better leader because of the commitment I've made to pay attention to my emotions and to open up what I'm feeling to the Father. Jesus, the ultimate man, modeled emotion. He laughed, He loved, He wept, He stressed and He even got incredibly angry. If the Son of God didn't suppress His emotions, why should I? When we, as men, take ownership of what we feel and get vulnerable with the Father, we become more like our Savior. We grow. We reap the reward of living a whole life.

PURSUIT

CULTIVATING A HEALTHY DATING RELATIONSHIP

"Every good and perfect gift is from
above, coming down from the Father of
the heavenly lights, who does not change
like shifting shadows." James 1:17

off the

HO
OK

Recipe for Overcoming Idealism —— Lindsay Vance

I spent the years leading up to marrying Zac uncovering a mess of romantic ideals. Some ideals I assumed from the marriages I grew up around. Some ideals I created when I misjudged how easily others fell in love. And still I agreed to carry more ideals as a way to protect my heart because I didn't want to fail. *Don't fall in love unless you know he's the one. Don't kiss him before you're engaged. If he doesn't have the right answers to your spiritual questions, he won't know how to lead you. God will tell you if he's the one. Everyone must like him. He must be perfect.* Zac had a lot to live up to when he picked me up for our first date. He and I would never have achieved a thriving love and marriage had my idealism won the fight. But thank God that perfectionism cannot stand in the face of Perfect Love. Love does not grow beneath the crushing weight of unrealistic ideals and expectations. Love grows in the vulnerable soil of the human heart, where it is free to make mistakes, change its mind and transform.

Romantic idealism blinds us from seeing the subtle ways love presents itself to us and crushes us when failure enters the relationship. For the first four months of our relationship, I wrestled underneath the weight of my desire for a perfect love story and God's perfect desire for me. In fear, I haphazardly posted rules on the entrance of my heart—ideals that I immaturely constructed to ensure that I would marry the right one. Rather than ask God to help me find balance between opening my heart and protecting her, I built walls of high ideals and hoped someone could jump high enough and cross over. I wanted Zac to adhere to my idea of a perfect love story through meeting my standards. For example, instead of feeling honored and celebrated when Zac asked me to be his girlfriend, I felt irritated because he asked "too soon." Idealism sold me the belief that I would have all the answers. When I didn't, I judged Zac for his inability to read my mind rather than take responsibility for my own questions and insecurities.

To risk falling in love is vulnerable, yet when so many of us enter into a dating relationship, we aren't prepared for the rigorous attention that vulnerability requires. Falling in love calls all our norms into question. It is risky to lay them on the line and possibly let go. For me, attention toward vulnerability meant setting aside vain excuses like "He must not be the right one" whenever I found fault with Zac. It meant allowing these moments of friction to instead serve as invitations to understand my heart and repent for ways I misunderstood love and the Lord. We want God to give us the answers and formulas to ensure a foolproof equation for romance. But God is so much more flexible than that. He knows that we don't look like Jesus when we demand perfection, but we become like Him when we love beyond imperfection. He believes in the fruit that the process produces. He wants to spend time teaching us, allowing us to fail and ask questions, guiding us as we wrestle through unavoidable pain and unexpected circumstances. This is how we learn who He is. This is how He wins our hearts. Dating is a joyous privilege that builds in us faith to trust God with one of the riskiest, most rewarding sources of joy in this life: marriage.

I remember the day when I took the risk and said "yes" to God's invitation to let go of my idealism. I bravely made the choice that my love story did not have to look like those of my friends and leaders around me. I didn't have to know that Zac was the man I was going to marry to let myself enjoy him. I remember laughing at his jokes freely instead of judging them. Maturity came when I let Zac off the hook of perfection and lovingly gave him space to be himself. As I let God remove layers of idealism, a willingness to press through moments of tension surfaced in our relationship. Temporary breakdowns did not mean that we were doomed to fail. It meant that we were destined to grow because we both wanted it. When I let go of a perfect standard, there wasn't this pressure for me to know all the answers, and Zac didn't feel like he had to prove something to me. We learned a higher standard—one of willingness, repentance and trust. We started having honest conversations, and we started having fun. In making mistakes, we grew in flexibility and forgiveness. We began to develop a new language between us where "I'm sorry" and "Will you forgive me?" were phrases that left us celebrating instead of feeling exposed. This language opened doors into our hearts that could never have been opened under the weight of idealism. Failure didn't define us; we were proud of our choices to bravely admit our faults and try again. We could feel God's smile, and we knew that He was proud, too. Slowly, we traded in foundations of judgment for foundations of open-handed communication and understanding.

Our love story is wholly imperfect. In the beginning we were fragile, confused and idealistic, but we were hungry for love and for God. The season of dating shaped our testimony. We fought hard to move against confining and controlling ideals in order to take hold of the freedom that is born in the fertile soil of vulnerability. It has produced a profound sense of purpose and an immense joy.

Prompt: Whether you're dating or you're single, you can begin to exchange your idealism for a vulnerable life in God. Ask God to show you where idealism has robbed you from experiencing His fullness. Where is He inviting you to trust Him and enjoy the risk rather than simply seeking a specific answer? Pray this prayer and journal His voice: "Father, I repent for demanding that love must come through for me in a certain way. Show me what it looks like to practice vulnerability in this season and stir up a joy within me that comes from a fluid, flexible life of trusting you."

CRACKING
THE
CODE

Recipe for Understanding the Myths and Reality of Dating ——— Havilah Cunnington

Artwork ——— Justina Stevens

I was a twenty-six-year-old virgin. I bought and read every book on sex, love, relationships and dating. I wanted to know, *How do I do this "relationship thing" God's way?* If that wasn't enough, I attended conferences, signed purity covenants and ran to altar calls looking for answers to the questions in my head. I didn't want to admit it, but I was desperate to crack the code. I always thought it was interesting that God put relationships in our lives we didn't choose, like our parents or siblings. Simultaneously, God gave us the free will and responsibility to choose one of the most important relationships: the partner we will hopefully have for the rest of our lives.

The night I met my husband Ben, the love of my life who I affectionately call my Baby Maker, was extraordinary. Sitting in a Chinese restaurant, we lost ourselves in conversation. It was easy. Simple. But when we started dating, things got more complicated. It wasn't that easy after all. The deeper and more committed we got to the relationship, the harder it became. Looking back I can pinpoint some of those complex reasons, the first one being the picture I had in my head of my one-day husband. I didn't want to admit I had a very clear image of my future partner. It wasn't a rough sketch but a very ornate, complex and colorful collection of images. When I wasn't nurturing a romantic relationship, I was busy adding to the big picture. When I finally met Ben, I had to spend an enormous amount of time deconstructing those images. Fantasy was easy, but the one I fell in love with did not match my pictures at all. I did discover reality is much more fulfilling and lasts a whole lot longer.

Also, I had to deal with the picture other people had for me. Living as a single woman in the world was everything but easy. My greatest fear was being left on the sidelines of the life I so desperately wanted. When I finally found the love of my life, I was surprised to find some skepticism from people. Words like, "I always thought you'd end up with…" and "Are you sure he's the right one?" made it very confusing for me. Knowing what your heart wants and hearing God's available voice is vital to a healthy relationship. Only you will be able to know and discern if this is the right relationship for your journey.

Lastly, I didn't fully realize that relationships aren't "One Size Fits All." Relationships are living and breathing connections. They are diverse, like snowflakes. It's impossible to take someone else's relationship and mirror it back to yours. It's best to look for ways to build similarities, enjoy the uniqueness you each bring to the relationship and give yourself grace to learn. It doesn't have to be perfect to be beautiful; perfect doesn't exist.

The journey to a lasting partnership can be scary and somewhat daunting. The pressure we put on ourselves and the pressure we feel from others can be complicated to navigate. People ask "brilliant" questions like, "Why aren't you married?" Instead of screaming in response, you can reply, "That's a great question. If I had the answer, I probably wouldn't be single."

I want to encourage you with this. While you're walking out your dating season, here are a few things to keep in mind: Community is important. Girls, stay close to your girlfriends. Guys, stay close with your guys. It is wise to be connected to a community around you before starting a relationship, whether it's through your church, a small group, your family or your close friends. It's important to not do life alone. In dating, it's so easy to get caught up in your own world of just you and the other person. To help with accountability and staying healthy, keep investing time into your closest friends.

Don't let your heart and emotional connection go deeper than your commitment level. At the beginning of a dating relationship, keep it low-stakes. If he's asking you out to coffee, he's asking you out for coffee. You're not signing a marriage certificate. As the relationship develops into greater commitment, open your heart to greater connection emotionally. Don't let your emotional excitement overtake your deep-down convictions God has given you.

Finally, your "no" is your "yes." If you're not feeling it, let the person know. Keep it real. Communicate. Show honor by not stringing them along. Your "no" to someone today is your "yes" to your future spouse tomorrow. Your "no" to being moved by emotions today is your "yes" to walking in wisdom tomorrow. Your "no" to crossing boundaries today is your "yes" to walking in purity tomorrow.

Dating should be a time of fun and discovery. You have the opportunity to get to know a person who has a whole different life experience than you. A time to understand their strengths and weaknesses, their uniqueness and creativity. Get to know them. Go on adventures. Ask questions. Have fun!

Prompt: Ask the Lord, "Father, give me your truth and clear thinking to make honoring and healthy choices in my dating season. What are the things I'm believing about dating that are built on fantasy, self-reliance or lies? Where do you want to dismantle the wrong beliefs and upgrade the way I see my single and dating seasons?" Journal His voice.

GOING BACK TO GO FORWARD

An Interview on Setting Healthy Boundaries with Luke & Rosemary Skaggs

By JD & Erin Gravitt / Photograph by Ginny Corbett

Luke and Rosemary Skaggs are an extraordinary couple in our Cageless Birds community who have been married for two years now. Luke played with Jonathan and Melissa's band off-and-on before coming to the 18 Inch Journey in 2013 followed by an internship with Joel Case in the Music Studio. After being on staff for a year, he has recently transitioned to working as a barista at The Table Farmhouse Bakery in Asheboro, North Carolina. He has a passion and great authority in the realm of music, instruments, producing and recording with other musicians. Rosemary was an 18 Inch Journey student in 2011 and completed our Phase II School in 2014, followed by an internship with Justina Stevens in the Leather Studio. Since then she has been a part of our staff, managing the Leather Department, leading worship and discipling students.

On a cold, winter's night, we had the opportunity to visit their light-filled, cozy home and interview them about their remarkable season of dating. Amidst a home bursting with creativity, instruments and art, we sat down and heard them tell their story with vulnerability and power. As you read their honest perspectives, may you feel permission to reach back in your own history in order to move boldly forward with the Lord and community.

TELL US ABOUT HOW YOU FELL IN LOVE.

LUKE: A mutual friend suggested we start a wedding music business together, and since we were both frustrated about not making money as musicians, we went for it. We got a website and professional photos taken. We started practicing and playing music.

ROSEMARY: I was really just in it to date Luke! I'd had a crush on him since I was sixteen years old when I first saw him at church. The ironic thing is we never played at a wedding together until after we got married!

LUKE: I started developing real feelings for her and finally told her very romantically on top of Pilot Mountain. We did everything so fast up front, but we dated for three and a half long years before getting married.

WHAT WAS THE TRANSITION FROM DATING ALONE TO DATING IN COMMUNITY LIKE?

LUKE: When we were first dating, it was normal for us to spend a lot of alone time together. We really didn't have any other friends. When we got to A Place for the Heart, our leaders had this amazing talk with us. They celebrated our friendship and who we were, but also brought up boundaries. We had no idea what that word meant. Boundary in my mind meant, 'Do not have sex.' They brought up things like time boundaries, physical boundaries and emotional boundaries. Because our boundaries were all over the place, we had to establish some brand new norms.

ROSEMARY: Our relationship went from a place of being really heavy and complicated—lots of heavy and long conversations and being really isolated—to something opening. Life, laughter and joy came back when we stepped into community and received leadership.

LUKE: It was hard and rocky those first few months, because I didn't really know how to relate to guys. When I got to A Place for the Heart and started living with the Phase II guys, that was a season of deep healing for me; I really hadn't been in healthy male friendships before this.

CAN YOU SHARE A TIME WHEN LACK OF BOUNDARIES CAUSED HEAVINESS? HOW DID THE LORD HELP LIFT THAT?

ROSEMARY: I dealt with a lot of heaviness and depression my whole life. I'd go to Luke to process my emotions before I went to the Lord. That created so much pressure and codependency. I would expect so much from him and when he couldn't give that to me it would cause frustration in my heart. Also, crossing physical boundaries caused so much shame. A relationship shouldn't have to feel confusion and shame, but we didn't have leadership. We opened up the topic of marriage way too soon into our conversations—only three months into dating! I put even more pressure on Luke to get married; I felt disappointed and upset when that marriage season didn't come quicker. Also, I struggled with codependency in male relationships before Luke and I started dating. Overcoming codependency with each other during dating happened when I realized that I had a deep need to be fathered by the Lord. That was eye-opening for me, receiving God's fathering, affirmation and strong presence. I was looking to Luke to meet that need, when I really needed the Father. I had experienced rejection in past friendships, especially from girls, and that created a deep need for love and affirmation in me. It seemed easier to hang out with guys or Luke all the time. A huge space in my heart started getting met through my female friendships in community—affirmation, joyful experiences, being known, opening my heart to them so they could help me. That lifted a huge weight off of Luke. My needs got put in their proper place.

LUKE: Most of my life there's been this thing that has needed to perform to be loved. When I hung out with guys I felt like I might not be accepted. With girls, I didn't feel competition; I felt unique or special. In my relationship with Rosemary there were places I felt really accepted, wanted, special and believed in, and those were places that I was actually yearning for community and male friendships. I wanted to be loved, but I was scared. Instead, I traveled with bands and performed in front of audiences for the feeling of acceptance or celebration. At church or with the band there's an immediate need being met of being seen and appreciated. I was dying to know that the Father actually loved me and saw me. I carried a lot of shame in our relationship, and there were deep needs I had that weren't met until I received fatherly affirmation in healthy community.

COULD YOU NAME SOME KEY THINGS THAT HELPED RESTORE YOUR DEFICIENCIES IN DATING?

LUKE: The first thing we needed was awareness. We were so unaware of what was happening. We felt shame and red flags in our inner worlds, but we didn't even have clear communication with the Holy Spirit. We didn't believe the best about Him or ourselves. So, sitting with our leaders was like the lights coming on in a house. Great leaders will tell you the stuff that's going on in your life that you had no idea about. I needed help badly because I'd prematurely brought up marriage, so I had to back-pedal in order to move forward. I had brought up the marriage conversation to feel secure in our commitment, but after six months of dating went by, I realized I actually didn't want to be married then. I wanted to be married to Rosemary one day, but I wanted personal growth and a relationship that felt joyful first. So, my leaders helped me gain language to communicate assurance of my commitment to Rosemary. I told her, "I'm not going back on what I said to you, but I did say it too early." I needed confidence to know I had what it takes to lead our relationship. I'd been walking in passivity and manipulation trying to make it work, but the men in my community helped me get through that. The more healed we became the more I had clearer vision for what it would take for me to get to a place to marry Rosemary.

ROSEMARY: A big key for me was softness. The Lord was able to do so much with our story and relationship because we were ready to ask for help and ask questions. Whether you have a game plan or not for boundaries in dating, if you are soft and humble, the Lord can help you and you'll be okay. For anyone dating, please don't be a know-it-all. It's a norm in our culture for young people to jump right into dating. You are setting yourself up for success when you are soft and ask for help. Our leaders were giving us the hard, honest truth, and we didn't buck up against it—we received it. It brought us so much joy!

HOW DID GOD GIVE YOU BACK YOUR RELATIONSHIP?

LUKE: On a practical level, we stopped over-processing with each other about things. Like, sometimes when we'd drive in the car together and start processing our days, it would start to get heavy. Part of it was wanting to talk out all of our struggles or problems right then and there. But instead, we started to keep each other accountable on dates saying, "Hey, I actually need to talk to the Lord about this issue right now, not you." Instead of over-processing, we would just

stop our conversation to pray. We learned that God's not anxious and wanting us to figure out our feelings right away. The Lord wants u to enjoy each other, and then we can talk to Him about whatever' bothering us another time. When we were dating, Rosemary had a lo going on in her inner world and I felt like I could help. It felt so goo knowing that I could help her figure out her problems. In my family our normal is that when someone needs help, you drop everything an help them—not necessarily in a peaceful way, but just in a rushin way. Anxious pressure sometimes led me; that was the image I had o the Father. If there was a problem happening, I felt like the Fathe wanted me to quickly do something about it, but I learned the Fathe isn't like that. I could be at peace in problem solving.

WHAT FRUIT ARE YOU SEEING IN YOUR MARRIAGE AS A RESULT OF ALL YOU HARD WORK IN YOUR DATING SEASON?

LUKE: I'm so thankful for what I learned in dating about givin Rosemary space and not figuring things out for her. We are here t support one another, but we are not here to fix everything. This yea has been challenging for me, because I've transitioned from workin at A Place for the Heart to The Table, a local eatery. Rosemary' been the biggest support for me, but she's never once felt anxiou about trying to figure out my transition. Even though we are ma and wife, there is One who is even closer. Knowing this is bringin so much joy and life in our marriage.

ROSEMARY: I am seeing laughter, joy and friendship. Having health physical and emotional boundaries in dating helped us commi to friendship and camaraderie. God gave us so much laughte instead of tears in moments of hitting walls. I'm also seeing th fruit of patience; we kept taking the Lord's invitation to wait to ge engaged. We followed His timing, and God helped us build stron foundations in our hearts and in our relationship. God saw ahead t all the building blocks we would need for our marriage in our datin season. We got to work that out with leaders and the Lord. Ther is now so much healing and a double portion for us.

WHAT'S A WORD OF ADVICE YOU WOULD GIVE TO SOMEONE WHO WANTS HEALTHY DATING RELATIONSHIP?

LUKE: Don't be afraid to seek help. We wouldn't be together withou the help of so many people. If I hadn't been around incredible me in my life, having conversations with them, walking the paths the walked, then Rosemary and I wouldn't be together right now. W aren't meant to date in isolation; I needed men who wouldn't coddl me when I made mistakes. Instead of saying, "Oh, it's okay, Luke. W all do that," the men in my life said, "You are forgiven, but we need t talk about this. If you allow this to stay a pattern in your life, thes will be the outcomes..." There was so much grace, mercy, joy an covering, but they didn't excuse me. For any young men, find olde men in your life that will give you the truth, even if it's hard to hear.

ROSEMARY: Overall, there should be an overarching sense of joy i a dating relationship. Dating shouldn't feel overly complicated o pressurized. The Trinity wants to be present to help in the mids of dating, especially in the ordinary, mundane moments, but als the more complex moments. The Holy Spirit is always accessibl and ready to help you!

IN JESUS' NAME

Short Prompt for Inviting the Holy Spirit into Dating ——— *Jonathan David Helser*

There are two inscriptions inside my wedding ring. The first is the date of our wedding and the second simply says, "In Jesus' name." This simple phrase has such deep meaning for us. It began when Melissa and I were dating. I was spending time with the Lord one afternoon before a date and the Lord began to speak to my heart from the verse in Matthew 18:20 (NIV): "For where two or three gather in my name, there am I with them." I had never thought about that verse related to marriage, but as I was reading that day I saw that marriage could be a place where this verse could be fulfilled 24/7. All it takes is two hearts joined in His name and they become a dwelling place for His presence. So, when Melissa and I got in the car for our date that night, I looked at her and said, "What if we invoke this promise that Jesus made anytime we go on a date—that wherever two are gathered in Jesus' name, He is there?" And so it has become a beautiful tradition for any date, even now, that we look at each other in the eyes and say, "In Jesus' name." This was more than a magic prayer or a formula; it was a value for the presence of Jesus to be the center of our relationship.

The question a lot of young people ask us now is, "How do I know if someone is the one?" This value for the presence of Jesus to be our priority is what really led Melissa and I in navigating this question. I can remember asking the Lord the same question, "Lord, is Melissa the one I am going to spend the rest of my life with?" The Father answered me with this thought, "Jonathan, if the closer you get to Melissa, the closer you get to me and if the closer you get to me, the closer you get to Melissa, then you know you are on the right path." A key to knowing your heart toward someone else is to make yourself aware—to stay sensitive to His presence. If growing in love with someone means growing in God, and growing in your relationship with God produces more love in your heart toward that person, you are moving in the right direction.

Prompt: How can you be intentional to invite Jesus into your dating relationship? Brainstorm ideas with the Holy Spirit of how you can evaluate your relationship in a healthy way. Are you growing toward God as your relationship is growing?

the God Card

Recipe for Owning Your Feelings ——— *Melissa Helser*

I love dating. I think it's one of the most fantastic seasons of a person's life. I love watching the sheer joy and excitement of what risk does to the human heart. Risk has a way of reaching down into the deep places and bringing all of a person's courage up to the surface. It is evidence of value and self-worth; the belief that you and your dreams matter to the Father.

I've been discipling young adults for years. I get to watch them pick up that courage and trust their hearts, and I consider it a great honor. It is stunning to behold. Full of tension and struggle, perseverance and victory, awareness and honesty. Taking a risk on your heart and getting to know another person is marked by courage and bravery. Valuing yourself enough to say, "I'm worth the

risk, even if it doesn't work out," is to say, "I trust you, God. I trust you to cover my heart."

Dating is amazing, and often difficult—it doesn't always work out. Over the years, I've counseled several young adults through all kinds of difficult dating scenarios, and I've realized a common thread in many of their dilemmas: they like to blame God for the way they feel.

Many of them feel overwhelmed by confusion and are so afraid of missing God's plan for their life that they end up in cycles of anxiety or depression. The joy of dating is gone, and often it's because they are too afraid to simply admit how they feel. By avoiding ownership of their emotions, they become paralyzed by fear and unable to make confident choices. Instead of acknowledging their need for change, they look for an excuse to validate their difficult choice.

I want to be clear: there is nothing wrong with recognizing a need for change for your heart. In fact, that is beautiful awareness, particularly in seasons of dating. But I find that when a need for change comes, it is more common for people to blame their change of heart on God instead of simply taking ownership for how they feel. We don't want to be responsible for causing pain, and since God is invisible, mysterious and all-knowing, many of us tend to blame Him for our break-up or use Him to validate our choice. This is a great tragedy because it paints a false image of God that distorts His nature. I call this unfortunate scenario the God Card.

Let me paint a picture to illustrate this dilemma: Elizabeth and John have been dating for six months, but John is beginning to feel irritated with Elizabeth. As he's grown to know her, he's realizing that although she's a beautiful and interesting woman, he doesn't want to spend the rest of his life with her. But because the two have grown in friendship, John doesn't want to be the one that causes Elizabeth's pain. So he looks for the easiest way out.

The two meet up to talk and he says something along the lines of: "Elizabeth, you're a great girl. I really don't want to break up with you but I feel like God is telling me to." Or, "I just feel like God is calling me into a season of singleness and I have to break up with you." John just played the God Card.

The God Card is the ultimate break-up trump card. It leaves no room for the other person to process or figure out how they feel. In this scenario, Elizabeth has no space to ask any questions, because all of a sudden, she's in a "God-told-me-so" moment. Who can argue with God? John has left Elizabeth with zero space to process her own feelings and opinions, and has ultimately robbed her of the closure process of their relationship.

In the meantime, God *didn't* tell John to break up with Elizabeth. God gave John a choice, and John has been given the freedom to choose what he loves and wants. God didn't put the pressure on John to make the perfect choice—He didn't threaten John or manipulate him into changing his mind. When John denies the fact that he has simply changed his mind, he undermines his own value and worth to God. This kind of language is full of passivity and is blaring with the belief that if John doesn't choose perfectly, God will punish him. John isn't being honest with his own heart or with Elizabeth,

and in his denial, he's painting a distorted image of God that sets both of them up to misunderstand His nature. John walks away full of self-righteousness and Elizabeth leaves feeling like God abandoned her or, at best, that she doesn't hear God's voice the way John does.

This is not to say that God never invites people out of the relationships they're in. Sometimes He does. He is God and He can offer any invitation He wants. When God invites people into a season of singleness or out of an existing relationship, that's beautiful. However, we must be careful to preserve the fact that God is extending a choice, not forcing us into what He wants out of control and manipulation. In this scenario, if God has invited John into a season of being single, he can communicate that without blaming God. If John's simply not into the relationship anymore, he should feel empowered to be kind and honest. In either scenario, John can own his feelings by saying something like, "Elizabeth, you're an amazing woman. I have experienced a change of heart. I don't want to be in this relationship anymore. I realize that my change of heart could hurt you and I'm really sorry." In this form of communication, John is taking responsibility for his feelings and change of heart. He's not painting a negative picture of God or setting Elizabeth up to feel like God has robbed something from her. And most importantly, John is not taking God's name in vain. In John taking full responsibility for his own feelings, he's leaving a clear pathway between Elizabeth and God for her process.

Whether you're single or dating, I want to charge you to take responsibility for your emotions when you communicate with someone. Pay attention to what your words are communicating about the heart of the Lord. Are you blaming Him when you don't want to hurt someone else? Are you putting words in His mouth instead of trusting Him to speak to the other person for Himself? Are your words driven by fear and panic instead of dreaming and value? You are capable of clear and powerful communication that speaks of value for your own heart and the hearts of those you share with. Take ownership and allow yourself to be empowered in how you communicate.

Prompt: Get to a quiet place with God and humble your heart. Ask Him: "Father, where have I made assumptions about your will and your character for the dreams in my heart? Will you speak into the places where I would rather blame you instead of hear what you have to say?" Allow His kindness and His conviction to wash over you. Journal His voice.

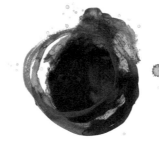

the gift of my

"For the Spirit God gave us does not make us timid, but gives us power, love and self-discipline." II Timothy 1:7, NIV

CHOICE

Recipe for Receiving the Risk of Dating as Gift ———— *Jessie Miller*

Artwork ———— *Justina Stevens*

"What about Chris Miller? Jessie, we really like Chris. He's just so great." Many raised eyebrows and smirks were coming my way, and I could hardly take it. I felt so frustrated and uncomfortable. Of course I noticed Chris! Of course I thought about him! But all my nervous hesitations were coming out in full force. "Protect, protect!" they cried. "Steer clear until you're sure! We've waited so long; he must be perfect!" I trusted these voices. They had kept me safe for so long. Yet I felt this stirring desire of possibility. My feelings toward Chris were growing, and I knew I was going to have to sort through them. Behind my walls of frustration, a fear was hiding: the risk of dating.

I've never been a fan of online shopping. You take a risk and order something you hope will be perfect. When it arrives, you critique it. If it doesn't fit or you don't like it, you have to send it back. So much decision, and so much hassle. I thought of dating the same way—so much risk! You find a guy, and then you see if it works. Even scarier, you try to decide if want to keep him forever. It felt so overwhelming. I was terrified by the power of my decision. I didn't want to mess up. It was much easier to dream about romance than to walk it out. Telling someone, "No, I'm not interested," or even worse, "No, I don't have feelings deeper than friendship for you," felt like a punishment. I hated when I hurt people and felt naive when people hurt me. I thought that if I was pursuing the right relationship, no one would get hurt or have to feel rejected. In my perfect world, God would simply send me someone who would immediately silence my nervous hesitations, and I would just know, "Here's my husband!" I wanted to make God proud, and in my mind that meant finding my life-long relationship without giving myself grace to practice or search.

Functioning under these filters, I tip-toed around dating for a long time. I did my best to spread out my longing for attention, commitment and interest. I tried not to take too much from any one person. This way no one could say I owed him anything, like my heart or the privilege to pursue it. I liked, I loved, I experienced and dealt rejection, but all of it was still at a reserved distance. And of course, there was Jesus. We had the most remarkable thing. My constant companion through the years. He cried with me through heartbreaks, dreamed with me and satisfied my soul in seasons where my longing for a companion could have swallowed me. My relationship with the Trinity was undoubtedly a romance. When thinking of having a boyfriend, and eventually a husband, a real question in my soul was, "What will happen to our love, Lord?" Would the Lord feel betrayed by a shift that might occur if I gave my heart to a man?

Over the following months my feelings toward Chris began to grow. A deep respect for who he was as a person was marking my heart, and my nervous hesitations began to be replaced with a new feeling—safety. I felt safe and championed in my interactions with Chris. Chris had a brilliant confidence about him that calmed me and often left me stunned with wonder. He was amazing. I felt like his relationship with the Father could sustain a season of us practicing our choice by dating, and furthermore I didn't feel the pressure to figure everything out on my own. On a crisp fall morning, several months after meeting and interacting, Chris invited me on a walk. Sitting by a very special lake, Chris asked for permission to intentionally pursue my heart. I said yes to a season of dating where we would discover what our lives held for each other. I decided to take the risk.

I had journaled that very morning before Chris and I took our fateful walk, and I felt the Father bring the most remarkable sense of release. He spoke this phrase: "The leaving of summer brings fall." It was time for me to embrace a changing of seasons. He spoke to me with a deep love and humility that poured from our years of intimate connection. He reminded me of a conversation we had during the year prior when I traveled through Italy embracing a season of glorious singleness. He whispered to my heart on an Italian vineyard, "It won't always be like this; someday beloved, I will share you." The time had come. He told me that He wanted to give me a gift, a gift that wouldn't fulfill all my needs, but would fulfill the desires of my heart. The Father's voice filled me with courage; there was no fear of betrayal in Him. He was full of compassion and excitement. He was not afraid of my choice. In fact, He was encouraging me to practice being brave, to "order the gift" and just see! The Father trusted me more than I trusted myself. He was not offering my relationship with Him as a reason to avoid taking a risk on love. I decided to embrace the gift of my decision instead of running from it. As it turns out, not only did I like my choice, but I fell deeply in love with him. On the other side of my fear was the most incredible gift.

Prompt: God loves to let us make choices. It is a privilege to make decisions, a gift to be cherished. When it comes to dating relationships, where are you afraid to make a powerful choice? Ask the Father to reveal what lie is holding you back and to give you His perspective on how to move forward in confidence and bravery. Pray, and journal His voice.

into the wilderness

Recipe for an Extravagant Dating Season ——— JD Gravitt

Artwork ——— Lindsay Vance & Morgan Campbell

When I asked Erin out it was a big risk for both of us, because neither of us had really dated before. She gave me permission to pursue her heart and I was ecstatic! She was far out of my league and had said yes to me! I was so validated by her choice that I became unbalanced in my identity. This was the most important thing about me. So you can imagine how devastated I was when just over a month into dating, we broke up.

This break-up began a year-long conversation with the Lord. The Lord invited me into the wilderness to show me *me*. I didn't know how to be okay with myself if Erin didn't choose me, which also meant I didn't know how to be okay with myself if she *had* chosen me. I needed a deeper revelation that I was chosen by the Father before I could be chosen by a woman. During one particular low moment of this year-long journey, the Father spoke to me and said, "I have you on the fastest track to the desires of your heart." He was taking me and my desire for marriage seriously, and there were things in my life that I needed to deal with. I had a choice to stop listening to the lies I was believing about myself. I faced these lies head-on by deciding not to get into any romantic relationship for six months. This decision helped change my mindset; I felt liberated from my own mind's constant attention to what other people might think of me.

Erin and I started to see each other more and more in our gatherings of friends. I had a new confidence as a man, because I had something to offer, not something I needed from her. I found myself with a new opportunity. Our friendship was growing again and I could tell that she liked me. Something that I had wanted for over a year was now back in front of me, and I was in a position to have it without it having me.

At the end of my six-month commitment, I took Erin to dinner and asked again if I could pursue her. She joyfully said yes, and it was game on! This time it was different. I was confident that my value didn't depend on her answer. I knew that I had a lot to bring to the table, and I knew that I was worth her time. I was also genuinely willing to walk away, because I was so content being single; dating was an added bonus. If this wasn't going to work, I wanted to find out sooner than later. With my new posture, our love had so much space to grow. I always felt intentional, but my level of extravagance grew with the level of our love. My expression of love matched the genuine love in my heart. To be honest, I didn't want to miss an opportunity to express my love for Erin, whether that was driving a lawn mower across town to her house to cut her grass or learning how to do something she loved, like swing dancing. I wrote letters, made photo books and cooked homemade meals.

For one of our first dates, I planned a whole "Day of Extravagance" for us to spend together. I sent a handmade invitation to her a week in advance. Then we spent the day exploring the city, going to museums, getting sushi and going to an outdoor summer movie. Six months later for Valentine's Day, I really wanted to do something special for her. I set up paper lanterns in a field and hung candles in mason jars from a tree. In order to pull this off, I enlisted help from my friends. I took Erin to dinner that night, while friends helped light candles, decorate and set up the scene. I blindfolded Erin and drove her to the field. Nat King Cole sang in the background as I walked her to the edge of the field to unveil my surprise.

The beauty of dating is that you get to create moments for your hearts to respond to each other. You have the opportunity to get creative with what's in your heart. A little bit of intentionality can go a long way. I won Erin's heart through diligence and consistency. I knew that I liked her and I took every opportunity to show it. Listen to what's in your heart, and be authentic in your expression of love.

Prompt: Maybe you're in a relationship or you're about to start one. My charge to you is to let the Father be intentional and extravagant with you first. Let Him solidify your value and worth before anyone else. Ask the Father, "What's one area of my value that you want to validate? How do you want to express the extravagance of your love to me?" Journal His voice. I challenge you to be intentional. Take the love you've received from the Father and put it into action. You have what it takes. Let your love grow. Even if it is just a spark, you can express your intentions in an extravagant way.

WHITE OAK
cut from the woods of Sophia, NC
approx. 90 years old

POTATOES AND PONIES

"Don't be misled: No one makes a fool of God. What a person plants, he will harvest. The person who plants selfishness, ignoring the needs of others—ignoring God!—harvests a crop of weeds. All he'll have to show for his life is weeds! But the one who plants in response to God, letting God's Spirit do the growth work in him, harvests a crop of real life, eternal life" (Galatians 6:7-8, MSG).

My crush on JD made me feel lighter than air. I was initially drawn to him because he was a deep well of no-nonsense confidence in Jesus. I saw a man of quiet strength, who didn't take easy shortcuts, but diligently worked hard in every area of his life to emerge from the fire unscathed, refined, victorious. I almost jumped the gun to beg him to consider dating me; I was ecstatic when he finally asked me out. JD, too, was drawn to the dancing flame of my peppy optimism—the rainbow rays of my extroverted personality made a way for bright light to infiltrate his pensive world. Serious practicality was merging with buoyant delight, and it was a doozy.

After a year of dating, the patterns were clear. JD tended to initiate conversations that were rich in depth, serious matters of the heart wrought with passion, deep thought and sometimes tears. My default in our times spent together was to maximize and capitalize on fun—carefree, playful, lively, wild, adventurous fun. On top of our lopsidedness in balancing the general mood of our relationship, we needed help figuring out the pace of dating. We wondered, *When is it an appropriate time to talk about marriage?* JD had brought up the topic several times, but I wasn't ready to fully think about switching gears. *And how should we let external pressures from parents, friends and family influence our pace?* People who we loved and who loved us had a lot of questions and wanted to know the answers to things about our relationship we didn't even know! It felt overwhelming and heartbreaking sometimes, the juggling of expectations, emotions and opinions on all sides. We loved each other deeply but needed insight on how to move forward so our love could progress in a healthy way.

Our saving grace came through the help of friends and leaders, who gave us language to own our connection and pace. We pictured our relationship like a cherished garden. Our garden needed a balance of both solemnity and playfulness in order to thrive and advance. Our garden needed JD's potatoes—hearty food to provide sustenance and justification for the journey. Our garden needed my peonies, too—technicolor flowers to add joy, energy and spontaneity. We learned to strike balance, so our needs could be met as a whole. "Potatoes and peonies" became our compass in the

months to come as we learned how to guide our conversations and time spent together. Quality time was spent playing mini golf with dear friends, getting a milkshake and a hamburger after a long day of work or watching episodes of our favorite TV show just to belly laugh together. Other moments were weightier, carrying thoughtful words exchanged about families, hopes and dreams, fears and prayers. This newly balanced back-and-forth gave our relationship an increasing sturdiness that confidently carried us through our engagement and to our wedding day.

If and when you are in a dating relationship, your garden—the pace and connection you are cultivating and harvesting together—will look different than anyone else's. Invite leaders and friends you trust into the garden of your dating relationship to help in the process; this vulnerable show-and-tell linked with honest, loving feedback helps the strong qualities of your relationship increase while plucking out weeds that want to infiltrate. Be aware of allowing someone to have influence over your garden when he or she doesn't bear full understanding and care; casual, curious feet can stomp flat fragile seedlings that want to take a risk on love. Remember that root systems can't be seen, although trust, honesty and respect may be patiently growing and maturing underground. Your potatoes don't have to be harvested right now nor your peonies already bloomed for your garden to have value. Trust God with your connection and pace.

Prompt: Take time to imagine what your collective garden with your significant other might look like right now. What seeds have you sown in the soil together? What are you harvesting and enjoying now? What's still underground growing and developing? Are there flowers that bring lightheartedness and play? Are there hearty plants that bring substance and nourishment to both of you? Are the people you are allowing into your garden trustworthy and helpful?

Go find a spot with just you and the Lord to reflect on your romantic relationship. It's so good to have one-on-one conversations with the Father, to ask Him for His perspective, wisdom and guidance. Make a bullet-point list in your journal of the kinds of seeds you have planted and/or want to plant in your garden (i.e. selflessness, trust, respect, adventure, etc.). Make a second list of the kinds of weeds that may be growing that you want the Lord's help to pluck out. Then, journal a prayer of thanksgiving to God for how your relationship is growing; receive the Holy Spirit's guidance in how best to tend to it, so that you can harvest His fruit with intentionality and enjoyment.

Recipe for:
Becoming
a Good Gift

BE
com
ing

By: Allie Sampson

During my freshman year of college, I decided to try out several different campus ministries until I found one that seemed like the best fit for me. After a month or so of searching, I landed at a ministry that met right off campus and began spending all of my extra time there; meeting friends, plugging into a small group and participating in different events and programs they offered. As I got to know several other students, I was struck by how sincere many of them were. I specifically remember looking around one evening during my first semester and being moved by how many of my guy friends were genuinely pursuing and worshiping the Lord. I'd seen a lot of crazy things in my first few months of school, but this was by far the biggest culture shock I'd experienced. Back home, I hadn't known many boys my age who were passionate about Jesus, and if I was honest, I would've told you that I thought loving God was something that men grew into when they got to be my dad's age. I remember my heart being flooded with inspiration and vision for my life. I told the Lord, "*This* is the kind of guy I want to marry—someone who loves you with everything they have. I want one of your best." In that sanctuary, I heard His voice resonate in my spirit above the crescendo of the music. He said, "Allie, I want to give you one of my best, but right now, you are not the kind of woman I could entrust with one of my best. That's not who you are yet. But it is who you could choose to become." My heart sank under the weight of conviction. I knew He was right. There was no shame or disappointment in His voice, just an honest and loving Father who was full of possibility for my future.

When I look back on my history with the Lord, I find this moment tucked away fondly in my memory. His candid kindness stirred my sleeping heart. In that moment, I realized that I had spent my entire life dreaming and obsessing over what kind of wedding I wanted to have, what kind of guy I wanted to marry and the gift he would be to my life, but hadn't thought *once* about the kind of gift that I wanted to be to my husband. In my early college years, I would have told you that I wanted to marry someone who was passionate about Jesus, who was patient and persistent, who wasn't afraid to get honest before the Lord—but was I those things? I had invested so much energy into dreaming about the man I would receive that I never thought to invest into my own heart—to become a beautiful gift that he would be proud to welcome into his life.

This honest moment with the Lord sparked an incredible season of intimacy with God like I'd never known. My heart was motivated. I was determined to become a beautiful gift. My focus shifted from begging the Lord to give me what I wanted to investing my time and energy discovering who I was—really was—in the Lord. I began spending long hours in campus coffee shops with my journal and getting lost in dialogue with the Father in my tiny lamp-lit dorm room. I'd spend time between classes asking the Father questions and listening for His voice. Eight years later, these are still some of my fondest memories with the Lord. This is where I laid foundations that will serve me for the rest of my life. It was the first steps in me taking ownership of my own heart. I can confidently say that this season paved the way for me to start walking out of insecurity and into trust with the Father— something that will absolutely carry into any relationship I have, and certainly into my marriage someday.

Now, instead of dreaming about the ideal man, I invest my energy into dreaming about the kind of marriage I want and thinking through what that is going to require of me. What kind of person do I want to be for my husband? Kind? Supportive? Considerate? What kind of mother do I want to be for my children? Joyful? Forgiving? Compassionate? I don't have to be in a relationship or have children to dream into that. And I don't have to wait until I'm married to begin cultivating those things. In fact, if I take ownership of the life I want now and start sowing into that, the harvest will be ready when the time is right. I don't want to get into my marriage and need patience only to find I've not planted any in my heart. I can start growing countless rows of compassion now—I intend to plant joy as far as the eye can see.

I am more excited and hopeful for my future marriage than I have ever been. This isn't because I have everything figured out or because I've finally built the perfect list to reference every man I meet by. It is because I believe that I am the best version of myself that I've ever been. I believe that I am a good gift, and becoming a better gift daily. As I invest in my own heart, I invest in my future marriage.

Prompt: Close your eyes and breathe deep. Take some time to think about your future marriage and family. Allow your heart to be washed over with vision. What kind of husband or wife do you want to be? What do you envision being the mark of your marriage? What about your children—what kind of parent do you want to be for them one day? Imagine the legacy and values you can pass down. Jot down some notes along the way in your journal.

When your heart is full of clarity and hope, craft a one-page vision statement in your journal about what kind of spouse you will be, and a second one for what kind of parent you will be. Use powerful language: "I will" statements instead of "I hope to" or "I would like to be" statements. When you've finished writing them, find a place where your heart feels safe to declare these things, and read them confidently out loud! Enjoy declaring with your powerful voice who you are in the process of becoming. After you've read them both, pray: "Father, thank you that you are committed to my present and my future. Thank you that you are full of vision and dreams for my life. Holy Spirit, fill me with inspiration and practical ideas of how I can practice becoming a good gift in the season I am in. I invite you to coach me and lead me into becoming the best version of myself. Thank you for making me a good gift, and for the work you are doing in me."

PLEASANT

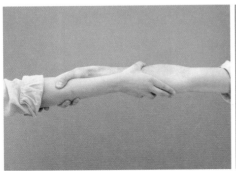

PLACES

"The boundary lines have fallen for
me in pleasant places; surely I have a
delightful inheritance."

Psalm 16:6, NIV

Erin and I worked very hard for our relationship. Neither one of us had really dated before, so I was full of intentionality for us. I had so much respect for Erin that I didn't think we needed boundaries for our physical relationship. I had never had a girlfriend that showed me physical affection and I expected the boundary lines to be self-explanatory like they were in any normal friendship. So, I was not prepared when the girl of my dreams wasn't off limits and she was choosing me back. We held hands and cuddled on the couch at first, but after a month into dating, physical boundaries weren't as obvious as I expected them to be. I thought I only needed boundaries for desires that were sinful. We were growing in trust with one another and becoming more comfortable with physical affection. We had to stop and recalibrate to define the physical boundaries we needed to sustain our relationship.

It's not enough to be passionate and dedicated to purity if we don't have a practical plan. Most of us have an intention to "save ourselves for marriage," but lack a practical plan for stewarding the freedom of dating someone beautiful and amazing. Our sex drive is a great gift from God and we need clear boundaries for our relationships to grow healthily. This takes honest self-assessment, input from community and assertive communication with each other. Everything is new in dating and our point of reference changes as we grow closer to our boyfriend or girlfriend. Defining physical boundaries helps us to navigate the pursuit of dating without losing our way. We have access to growing love and it's our responsibility to plan for its development.

Whether you're in a relationship or you're about to start one, I charge you to establish your physical boundaries at the beginning. When your relationship grows, your sex drive will increase and it's unwise and unfair to expect your willpower to hold you accountable. It's vital that you initiate a conversation with the Holy Spirit about your boundaries so that you don't leave room for interpretation or confusion between you and your significant other. This will give your relationship space to grow in safety and confidence.

Prompt: Invite the Holy Spirit to inspire you with vision for your relationship and help you set boundaries to steward your vision. Take out your journal and write down responses to these questions:

1. *Holy Spirit, what does it look like to honor you when I feel sexually triggered?*
2. *Read His response. Then ask Him for 1-2 simple boundaries you need to keep yourself in a safe, healthy place.*

Once you've sat with the Holy Spirit and feel clear on what would help you, sit with your boyfriend or girlfriend and share the boundaries you need. A great rule of thumb is this: if one of you feels conviction to avoid something, then both of you should honor that. Each of us have a unique sensitivity to the Holy Spirit and it is important to honor what each other needs. Together answer these questions so that you both are on the same page for what relating physically looks like in this season:

1. *What is your plan for watching movies together? What does honor look like in this scenario?*
2. *What is your plan for cuddling, hugging or massages?*
3. *What is your plan for alone time? Do you need a time limit, a curfew?*
4. *Do you plan to kiss and where is your stopping point?*

Write down the practical boundaries that you need to steward the freedom and purity of your relationship. Share this list with each other and the leaders in your life. Let hope and joy lead you in this process as you make a plan to achieve purity in your relationship.

the missing peace

Recipe for Redemptive Balance in Relationships ——— Justina Stevens

We're snowed in today. My husband is next to me looking at the weather update, my son fast asleep in his crib. I haven't seen a snow like this in years; the last time was when I was much younger, unmarried and full of all kinds of dreams for my future. I always wanted to get married and have a family. I grew up the youngest of four girls with a humorous father and a creative mother. I was sheltered. In my formative years I genuinely thought boys were odd, and if I developed romantic feelings for them I treated it like a cold or the flu—I got rid of it as fast as possible.

Those feelings scared me. They weren't concrete or tangible, just these "things" that lived in an invisible world looming over me and around me. As a teen and young adult, physical romantic relationships were simple enough to understand: *don't go past this boundary, don't kiss too long…etc.* But emotional boundaries?…that was a nameless vastness that I did not understand.

I didn't date until I was twenty. I walked hand-in-hand with my first boyfriend. He looked like my childhood dream: tall, blue eyes and blonde hair. Looking back, I want to shout to that girl, "Oh darling, what are you doing?" She was still a child mentally. I approached our relationship with lofty ideas of marriage within the first weeks of dating. I expected the world from him. I expected a Cinderella story. I couldn't believe how quickly he took interest in me, the attention I got. After the "tragic" end of our relationship I began to realize how fantastic male attention was and how easy it was to get.

I wasn't a fool. I wasn't going to start a relationship like I did with my first boyfriend—too messy. But, I could get the emotional attention my soul craved easily from men. I made several friendships with the opposite sex throughout college. We'd sit down alone for lunch at a restaurant, look into each other's eyes, tell jokes and make each other laugh, fill the air with intentionality…but *no, no, no, it wasn't a date.* We were "just friends."

Looking back, I didn't cognitively think to myself, *I will get what I want in this sneaky, unhealthy way.* In my immature mind these friendships just happened to me. I thought that if I didn't have feelings, they didn't; if I didn't have a problem staying in control of my romantic thoughts, my thoughts automatically controlled theirs. I thought I could share parts of my heart and play the heroic role when my guy friends needed consoling as long as my intentions were pure. I was foolish.

I never considered how my behavior affected my guy friends, never stopped to realize I led many of them to believe that I was interested in something I truly wasn't. I had set up an emotional cushion for myself to feel wanted, valuable and interesting. Twenty-two-year-old Justina didn't understand that boundaries were created to protect friendships, not end them. The greatest misunderstanding I carried was this: I truly believed that boundaries damaged me, my dreams and hopes. I never stopped to realize that boundaries were a gift God was waiting at the door of my heart to give me so that I could feel empowered and every dream of my heart could come true. Yes, I said every dream.

God gave me my longing for companionship, but I took these dreams and hoarded them, pushing out His wisdom because I was convinced He would take it all away. I couldn't stand the thought of being alone, but in actuality He couldn't stand the thought of me experiencing loneliness. God put every beautiful dream inside me as a road map to find Him, to find home. When my eyes were opened to what my behavior was actually communicating, I repented to the Father and I decided to change. It wasn't a "woe is me" prayer; I actually felt very privileged to be loved enough to see my immaturity for what it was. It felt amazing to take steps toward being a powerful person.

I began making good choices: I asked the Holy Spirit for sensitivity when I was pulling on people around me to feel full,

I asked my close friends for feedback from interactions they witnessed, I began carving out time for fun to fill my heart. If I felt like something was "off" between me and a guy friend, I asked the Holy Spirit if I needed to make an adjustment. It was hard work, and it changed my friend group dramatically, but I knew it would be worth it. As I pressed into wholeness I expected for things to get easier, but unfortunately, they didn't. I began to experience high levels of anxiety. I thought that perhaps I was doing something wrong, or not doing enough. One day, I sat down with a friend who was a bit older than me. I emotionally rattled off how hard I was working and my frustration that it didn't seem to be paying off. I received the best question in return, "Justina, where do you think this anxiety is coming from?" she asked. I paused and searched my mind, my heart. "I don't know…I think I've always felt like this, I just feel so behind, like I'll never catch up." In her simple question, the truth of what was going on in my heart was revealed: anxiety had always been there. My eyes were opened to the fact that anxiety was a trigger that led me to making bad choices in friendships as a way of coping with the overwhelming feeling of being behind. Feeling connected to a man emotionally was a temporary calming effect that would numb the anxiety. To my surprise, it wasn't about doing more or doing less, I needed to learn to walk through the pain instead of away from it, because on the other side of that pain were my dreams, my holy confidence, my balanced life. I chose to stay persistent. I kept asking for help, kept making powerful choices. I fought years to find me, and it was worth it.

I have by no means reached this imaginary "arrival point" that we all wish existed—that place all of us dream about, where we finally pray the right prayer or do the right thing and we somehow gain access to a worry-free, fail-free life; but I have learned a new rhythm of trusting the Father's direction. This new way will sustain me for years to come. Trust is not a spiritual gifting but the substance created in tension—in waiting and relying on God's fulfillment. It is never too late to build trust with the Father.

So I sit, on the oversized couch in my living room staring at the falling snow, feeling the redemption and incredibly proud of myself. I am sitting in the reward of making good choices and it feels great. All my should-haves, all my shortcomings and anxiety mysteriously have been covered and forgotten just like the ground has vanished under pure white.

Prompt: Take your journal and ask the Holy Spirit to bring one relationship to mind that needs His redemptive balance. It can be a friend, parent, boyfriend/girlfriend or spouse. Ask the Father, "Are there places in this relationship that I am leaning into to get affirmation that I can only get from you? Am I putting unhealthy pressure on my friend? Are they putting unhealthy weight on me?" Allow Him to respond. If you find that there is an imbalance in your way of relating, ask the Father one more question, "Father, what are some simple boundaries that will actually protect me and this relationship?" Once He's given you some ideas, share these thoughts with a leader or healthy friend; ask them for their feedback. Once you feel clear and full of joy, put these boundaries into practice with the relationship.

A DEBT IS NOT A GIFT

Recipe for Overcoming Entitlement ——— Joel Case

Artwork ——— Justina Stevens

Marriage had always been a dream in my heart, something I deeply desired and believed God truly had for me. My journey toward receiving this gift has been challenging and marked with questions, especially the five years right before I met my wife, Kateland. Being single and watching all of my closest guy friends meet and marry the women of their dreams left me confused, frustrated and unsure of God's heart. *Where was my love story? Why not me? Why not now?* In an attempt to make sense of the absence of my wish fulfilled, I leaned into idealism—the forming or pursuit of unrealistic standards. I reasoned that because it was taking longer and the road felt harder, the gift of my wife would be that much more amazing. In a way, I felt entitled to it.

I had been given so much encouragement from friends that my wife was going to be out-of-this world, but in my impatience, I interpreted that to mean that God owed it to me. A lack of trust was being exposed in my heart that God wasn't going to come through. To me, the dream of a beautiful wife wasn't a gift God freely wanted to give me anymore; it was a debt I deserved! In this way, beautiful hope became selfish, self-righteous entitlement. The unspoken, "God, You owe me," beneath the surface of my heart was like a faulty projector casting images of my own demands and fantasies of my wife and marriage, not the Lord's. These phantom ideas said, "If I can just have that kind of woman, I will be settled and fixed. I'll be rewarded." I was dreaming my own dream without yielding my failures, insecurities and deficiencies to God. I was so blinded by idealism and entitlement that, really, even the most "ideal" woman wouldn't have been enough. "She" wasn't the issue. The issue was in my own heart.

This "You owe me" I felt deep inside toward God not only cast a shadow on who deserved to marry me, but it cast a shadow on my friendships and on the way I viewed my leaders—everything! I had to come to terms with the reality of my imbalanced way of thinking and owned the fact that I needed help from God and the people around me. God wanted to meet me through the eyes of leaders that had gone before me, but that required me to humble my heart and be willing to hear the hard truth: that I seldom practiced gratitude and often took whatever I wanted, thinking of myself above those around me. What I learned in that season was that ungratefulness, comparison and jealousy had created a dam in my soul blocking out gratitude, clarity and connection with my Creator. Simply opening my heart to trustworthy people helped me more than I can express; being seen and feeling understood transformed my heart. From there, practicing gratitude for my one amazing life, for what the Father had done for me, for what He had given me lifted even more heaviness off my heart. I had to practice. I had great days and tough days, but gratitude moved me forward into brand new thinking and behaving.

I am so glad that God began a great work in my heart before I became friends with Kateland. I didn't see her through a veil of judgment; I was taken aback by her pure eyes and I could see the beauty of Jesus radiating from them. Her beauty was suddenly so attractive to me. My heart leapt at the chance to sit and talk with her; I really wanted to get to know her. Through it all I felt the wink of the Lord nudging me on, "Isn't she great?" He was just as excited as I was to find out what this new spark could be.

Grateful eyes don't demand perfection. In our image-based culture, where we can see pictures on social media of "perfect" meals, couples and houses, we perpetuate idolatry if we don't allow the Holy Spirit to heal our eyes and meet our needs. Seeing people and things with eyes of grace starts with seeing ourselves that way—through the eyes of the Father. This gives us a sense of beauty and thanksgiving, not comparison and fantasy. The cure for entitlement will always be gratitude.

Prompt: Have you held a grudge against God? Have you built a high expectation for your current life or the future to be a certain way? Take some time to meditate on areas of your life where you feel entitled. Then, hold your closed fists up in the air in front of you. Imagine that thing inside of your palms, and release it to the Father as you open your hands. Say to the Father, "I release this to you. Thank you for your good gifts."

LEGACY

CULTIVATING HOLY SPIRIT-EMPOWERED PARENTING

"Children are a heritage from the Lord, offspring a reward
from him. Like arrows in the hands of a warrior are
children born in one's youth."   Psalm 127:3-4

QUICK to Love

Recipe for Having Grace for Ourselves and Others ——— *Jonathan David Helser*

Photograph ——— *Melissa Helser*

Since my daughter, Haven, could walk, she has always loved to be in the kitchen making something. She loves to bake cookies, and when she does, you can see the evidence of her process all over the kitchen. Fingerprints of butter on the fridge, sugar crystals sparkling all over the floor and flour dusted across the kitchen like a light snow flurry passed over our home. I will always treasure these memories of her sticky hands and her happy heart baking in the kitchen, but there were a few times that, in the busy moments of life, a messy kitchen was quite inconvenient.

On one particular day I walked into the kitchen and was instantly overwhelmed at her baking expedition. I was exhausted after a very full day and we also had guests coming to the house that evening, so I really didn't want the kitchen to be a mess. She could feel my frustration brewing as I anxiously paced around the kitchen. In the middle of my frustration, I felt the gentle whisper of my Father speak to me, "Jonathan David, my son, I let you come into my house all the time and you have also made quite a few messes, but I never react to you in frustration. The way you are reacting to Haven will shut down her heart and creativity. You only have another decade with your daughter in your kitchen. Would you relax and enjoy these moments with her?" I treasure these teaching moments as a parent; when the perfect Father in Heaven steps into our world and teaches us how to love and parent like He does. I am so thankful God doesn't demand that we figure out parenting all on our own. He really does want to help us every step of the way.

After this beautiful correction moment from my Father, I took a deep breath, turned around and placed my hand on my daughter's shoulder and asked if I could talk to her for a moment. She put down her cookie dough and looked up into my eyes. I said, "Haven, I am so sorry I was frustrated and overwhelmed with you. I love your cookies and I love your passion to bake. It's my joy for you to cook and you always have permission to make a mess. Please forgive me for overreacting." Without a moment of hesitation she said, "It's okay Dad, I forgive you. Don't worry, I will clean the kitchen when I am done." Right at that moment the timer on the stove began to beep and Haven joyfully responded with, "Yeah! My first batch of cookies is ready! Dad, would you like to try one?"

I think these are some of our greatest parenting moments—when we humble ourselves in front of our kids and own our mistakes. It's not easy being vulnerable with our mistakes, but I believe it's worth it. I can look back on my early days of parenting and see how much I was performing to try and be the perfect dad. Everything changed when I realized I will never reach that unattainable goal to be the perfect father. There is only one perfect Father and that is our Father in Heaven. One of the greatest things I can do as a parent is to lead my children to the Father. I am constantly astonished at this responsibility and privilege to teach them who God is and what He is really like. I am also deeply humbled that my actions, my words and the life I live before my kids affects their perspective of who the Father is in a significant way. When I look back at that moment in the kitchen with Haven, I realize that those interactions have the power to mold her belief system. If I always react with frustration to the messes she makes in life, it could easily shut her heart down and even worse, begin to diminish her view of who God really is. I am so thankful the Father redeemed that moment in the kitchen. I want my children to remember my kindness, laughter and peace far more than they remember the moments of my frustration and impatience. As parents, we never arrive and have it all figured out. I think it's absolutely amazing that while I am in the midst of parenting my children, I am still in the process of being Fathered by God.

Over the last few years the Father has been going deeper into my own heart to get to the roots of performance and perfection that have caused me to react so strongly to mistakes. I have realized that the way I treated Haven's mess in the kitchen is a reflection of how I treat myself when I make mistakes. It is so true that we love others as we love ourselves. This truth will play itself out in our homes more than any other place. If I cannot learn how to release grace to myself when I make a mistake, I will have a very difficult time extending grace to those around me when they mess things up. It's not enough to tell my kids that it's okay to make mistakes if they watch me beat myself up when I make a mistake. What has brought significant transformation to my life is discovering who God really is and how He responds to the messes I make. As I have discovered how slow the Father is to get angry and how quick He is to love, I have been changed and my response to failure has been transformed.

In my journey toward wholeness, it has been incredible the way God has engineered circumstances in my life to work these truths deep into my heart. This one particular circumstance stands out as a significant defining moment for me in confronting this issue. It all happened when we took a special family trip up to the Blue Ridge Mountains in North Carolina. When we arrived at this beautiful old mountain lodge, I was looking for a parking spot and I didn't see a low rock wall around one of the corners. All of a sudden, I clipped the rock wall with the side of our van. I hit the wall so hard that whether I drove forward or backward, the rock just kept digging

deeper into the door of the van. This wasn't just a scratch; it was a massive dent in the door of our van. When I finally got the van free, Melissa and the kids sat in stunned silence, just waiting to see how I would react. They knew that the fate of the rest of that day was hanging in the balance of my choice. They have watched me in the past make a mistake and then spend the rest of the day beating myself up with guilt. I knew that I was in a defining moment; I was at a crossroad of whose voice I would listen to.

As a man, making a mistake like ramming my car into a rock wall will usually unleash the voices of shame like an army raiding a castle. I could feel the tide of negative self-talk rising: *I am so stupid. How could I not see that wall? Why do I always mess up a great day?* But in that moment I could hear another voice louder than all their noise. I heard my Father's still, small voice speaking to my heart: "It's just a mistake. Be kind to yourself. It's your privilege to make mistakes, because it is my joy to redeem them and to work all things together for your good." I knew it was time to evict the voices of shame, believe the truth of my Father's words and be kind to myself. I broke the silence in the car with this response: "Well guys, it's just a mistake. I didn't see the wall. It's just a car and this time in the mountains with you is so much more important than a car. This is not going to ruin our day." As these words were coming out of my mouth, the kids instantly started clapping from the back of the car with excitement and exclaimed, "Dad! Oh my gosh, we are so proud of you!" I looked across the car at Melissa and she was smiling with joy. She has watched me over the course of our marriage wrestle through this false belief system of perfection and performance and seen how I have treated myself when I fail. She knew I had just passed a test. The fruit of all this practice, this journey toward wholeness, is coming to moments like these and getting to celebrate my growth with my family. In this moment, we all knew I was being changed and becoming more like my Father in Heaven. A father who is slow to anger and quick to love.

Prompt: Grab your journal and ask the Holy Spirit to help you remember a moment in the past month when you were rude to someone close to you. Once a moment comes to mind, ask Him, "Holy Spirit, what am I believing about myself in moments like these? How does the way I treat myself affect others?" Give Him space to help you understand what is going on and journal His voice.

AN OBEDIENT YES

Recipe for Courageously Saying Yes ——— *Rita Springer*

Photograph ——— *Personal Collection*

"He predestined us for adoption to sonship, through Jesus Christ, in accordance with his pleasure and will" (Ephesians 1:5, NIV).

Adoption is on my mind all the time. It is thirteen years old and lives in my house. It is my heart walking outside my chest. When I think about adoption though, I cannot help but reflect on the life of Joseph. The Joseph who walked into a situation he didn't ask for and became an earthly father to a child not biologically his. He had an angelic encounter to prepare him for what was going to happen. He and his bride would not be married in the church of their choice or by the rabbi they wanted. They would not have a honeymoon or get excited together that they had conceived their first child. Joseph was asked to give his heart to a woman and father her unborn son. God had essentially asked him to adopt this Messiah and father Him. Raise Him up. Believe in Him. To look past the bloodline when the bloodline in Jewish culture was a pretty big deal.

I get asked a lot about how I adopted my son, Justice. I love the story because it isn't much different than the Bible ones. I wasn't ready to adopt anything. I was busy on the road, traveling every weekend, exhausted on the returns. I had been fasting and praying about finally being given a husband and starting a family. In many ways, I was begging God to show up personally and answer the desires of my heart first! As it turns out, I was holding a sick baby in a hospital in Romania when God asked me to adopt. It wasn't at all expected nor did it fit into my timeline. I panicked about the prospect of it. The encounter with God was so strong that I knew my obedience was what He was simply asking for. Eight months later, I nervously drove from my home in Charlotte, North Carolina, to Jacksonville, Florida. I parked at an Applebee's restaurant and waited for the woman who was carrying Justice. A week later, I walked into the hospital and stood by her side as she delivered my son. I had no idea the encounter I would fall into with God.

The moment Justice was mine and I drove away from that hospital, I felt the Spirit of God come in a way I had never felt before. It was as if I had stumbled upon Jack's magic beans and all I could do was ask the Lord a million questions about what was happening to my heart. Why was adoption so powerful a bond? It is exactly what God did for me. He gave me His name. He gave me ownership in His inheritance. When I looked at my baby's face, I could feel Jesus close. When I held Justice while he slept, I knew God was with me. In fact, God seemed to act like the new father who didn't want to go to work because he might miss a feeding or a diaper change. God was near. More than He had ever been. I had obeyed to do something so close to His heart that He, in return, stayed so close to mine. It was as if I had obeyed to turn a light switch on, and when I did, it lit up the whole world.

In our court system the bond between parent and adopted child is more iron clad than a biological bond. You can revoke your rights to your biological child, but you cannot when you adopt. Think about that from God's perspective. Our God can never revoke His right to be your Father. Galatians 3:29 says, "If you belong to Christ, then you are Abraham's seed, and heirs according to the promise."

My son is now a teenager. I am a wordsmith and yet when I try to tell anyone how I love him, I find myself speechless. When I see Justice, I see goodness and glory. I see honor and light. I hear God clearly and I marvel. What if I would never have responded? I would have missed the sound of God's voice. Joseph said yes, too. Isn't it breathtaking that it was Joseph, not Mary, who was in the bloodline of David that led to the line of Jesus! This Joseph simply said yes to adoption and the baby that changed everything.

Prompt: Whether you are single, married, or a parent, ask the Lord where He is inviting you into obedience. Where in your life is it time to respond? Where is He waiting to illuminate your world through your powerful yes? Journal His voice and engage your faith—take a courageous, obedient step.

FACE — to
— FA
CE

Recipe for Intentional Parenting ———
David Burbach

Photography ———
Sydnee Mela & Morgan Campbell

"I have no greater joy than to hear that my children are walking in the truth" (III John 1:4, NIV).

More often than not, my son is moving too fast for me to catch his eye. At five years old, he lives his life at a break-neck speed, running, climbing, and playing from dawn till dusk. I'm convinced that no one on earth is freer than a five-year-old in summer. When I do catch his eye, it's because I've pursued it. I catch him in the fury of his play and wait just a minute longer than he expects. In that moment I feel the strain go out of his body as he looks to me. "Yes, Papa?" My words say it's nothing, but my heart knows better. It is everything to look into my son's eyes for a brief moment to see him and have him see me. It can happen at bedtime, too. After reading a book and our nightly prayer, in the final moments of his restless fight against sleep, I make it a point to stare into those huge, blue eyes that look just like mine. *I want to know you.*

Of course, these are the parenting moments when all is good and right in the world. The moments when I've remembered that eternity exists and that I want to savor every moment I get with Gideon and his little sister, Winter Grace. But then there are other moments. Times when I'm short and angry with them, times when I'm in a rush to get somewhere or do something that's probably not as important as I think it is. Times when I miss out, and times when everything is going wrong. There's stress about money, about school, about work, about life, and it all eats away at the peace required to drink from the rivers of living water.

And then the realization hits that eighteen years only amount to 6,570 days. With Gideon, around 1,900 have already passed. Something in me wants to fight against this tyranny of time. *No!* My eternal soul screams. It's not enough. 10,000 years wouldn't be enough. It seems so wrong, so unnatural that life, and childhood in particular, should be so brief. Despite my wishes, time continues its inexorable march toward the day when either I'll breathe my last or trumpets will sound from on high. I want to make the most of the numbered days I have between now and then, and it starts with my kids.

It's easy to forget that in order to be a good father, I must first remember that I am a son. More than that, I must learn to be a son. It's not enough to think about it every once and awhile; I find that if I'm not constantly submitting to the grace and kindness of my heavenly Father, I quickly run out of grace and kindness for my own children. Without His love, I'm powerless to love them

well. Without His eternal presence permeating my life and my day, I tend to go on autopilot, checking off tasks with all the passion and efficiency of a robot. Therein lies perhaps my greatest fear—that when my wife and I find ourselves with an empty nest, I'll have performed all the functions of a parent without actually being a father. It may seem irrational, and perhaps it is, but nevertheless I feel the ever-present invitation to intentionality as a parent. To look deeply into my children's eyes and drink in their personhood. To get to know them before they even know themselves.

Blake Casteel, a good friend of mine, once said, "I don't know why married couples wait to have kids. They're just putting off discovering how the Lord really sees them." I was a newlywed at the time, and these words certainly gave me something to chew on. Now, seven years and two kids later, I feel like I'm just now beginning to understand what he meant. For the first time I'm beginning to understand what Brennan Manning calls "the furious longing of God," to know and be known by His children.[2] By me. As a father, I not only want to pursue my children and unravel who they are, I want to likewise open myself up to them. I want to invite them to see me struggle, and I will not hide my failures from them. Most of all, I want them to see me trust in and walk with Jesus.

On his blog, *Leading the Way,* Dr. Michael Youssef says, "When our children see us clinging to the promises of God, they will grow up trusting in His goodness. If we fail as adults in praying for and praying with the next generation, then they will become spiritually unsure."[3] When it's all said and done, quality time with God, my children, or anyone else isn't just about spending time together. It's about connection. It's about knowing and being known. It's about looking into each other's eyes and sitting in each other's presence. As a father, I've become painfully aware of the short time I have to discover who my children are and share who I am with them. As a son, I'm grateful that I have eternity to soak in the nature of God—but that doesn't mean that I want to waste a single day.

Prompt: Get face to face, eye to eye with your child, no matter how old he or she is. Stop, linger, savor. Ask the Father to overwhelm your heart with love for the gift of their life. Then, imagine the Father getting face to face, eye to eye with you. Ask Him, "Father, how do you love me?" Journal His voice.

ALL MY ————————

SONS

An Interview on Strategic Parenting with Matt & Debbie Peterson

By Allie Sampson & Erin Gravitt / Photography from Personal Collection

It's a crisp Sunday evening, just after dinner. The sound of the 18 Inch Journey students laughing in the Farmhouse carries through the office as excitement starts to surface in my heart. I've been looking forward to interviewing Matt and Debbie Peterson for a long time.

I've crossed paths with Matt many times. He regularly comes to teach during our discipleship schools and has been speaking into our community for years. Back in their ministry school days, Jonathan and Melissa were mentored by Matt, and he's become a spiritual father to the Cageless Birds community. Matt leads Awake Church in Winston-Salem, North Carolina where Debbie co-leads the children's and women's ministries. Matt is also an author and leads Hydrating Humanity—a nonprofit with a mission of bringing clean water, water hygiene and the Gospel message to those in need. Twenty-two years into marriage, Matt and Debbie have five sons ages thirteen to twenty-one, and have some incredible insight to offer on parenting. As you read this interview, may you be inspired by their journey with intentional parenting and encouraged to invite the Holy Spirit into your own rhythms of parenting.

TELL US ABOUT YOUR FIVE AMAZING SONS.

DEBBIE: Our oldest, Josiah, is twenty-one; he'll be graduating from college soon. He could've been raised by wolves! He picks up everything quickly and is very responsible. Then comes Seth, who is nineteen; he's a freshman in college and is the kindest person I know. Sam is eighteen and is the jokester of the family. He brings fun wherever he goes. John is sixteen and is very laid back. He has real inner strength. And Andrew is thirteen and is also so funny. He always makes us laugh. I was raised in a combined family with mostly boys—seven boys and two girls. I was raised with brothers, so it was an easy transition for me to be a mom of all boys.

OVER THE YEARS, DO YOU FEEL LIKE YOU'VE TRANSITIONED AND ADAPTED YOUR PARENTING STYLE?

MATT: We've had to parent differently based on each unique child and what they need. Of course, their teen years are completely different, too. In trying to find that balance, the greatest concern that we've had in their teen years is their relationship with God and the input that they're receiving. We've been like coaches to our sons, facilitating the atmosphere of the presence of God in their lives. But we can't make them read their Bibles and follow the Lord and all those things—we didn't want to push them away. We learned a lot through watching kids who have grown up in church; if they rebel, oftentimes it's because their parents were pushing God down their throat. Finding those balances and wanting to introduce them to experiences with the Lord on their own is probably one of our biggest challenges right now as parents.

CAN YOU SHARE A BIT ABOUT THE DIFFERENT APPROACHES YOU TAKE AS PARENTS DEPENDING ON YOUR SONS' PERSONALITIES?

MATT: When something like a behavior emerges in their lives—whether that's good or bad—those are teaching moments. Those are moments to begin a conversation. I think we try to take advantage of those moments as much as possible. If there are things in our culture that come up—like on the news—we try to grab and use that as an example for what's right or wrong. We want to encourage them to adopt God's values and our family's values. Those moments just emerge; sometimes you can't really plan them. We also try to have some family meetings every other week. We want everybody to be able to ask questions, and we ask them questions. We want to have a time where there's exchange, input and questions, so that we're dropping things in their hearts.

DEBBIE: We have family dinner as much as we can. It is the best way I know to catch up on the day. It is also a time to talk about everyday topics as Matt said. I keep a file where I write down life training topics we have discussed. I started doing this because I could not remember topics we

had discussed and who was there to hear it. For example, my kids like to swim in a deep water hole nearby. I had the thought, *They need to always check the water level (even though they are familiar with this spot) every time they go in just in case there is something that has drifted into the place they dive or the water level is down.* After we've talked about this, I write down the topic and who was present because it gives me peace and I do not bother my kids with telling them things over and over again, as moms can have the reputation of doing. When my kids are at the waterhole and I think, *Did we talk about...* I'll go check. Sometimes they'll say, "Mom, we've already talked about that." And I'm like, "Okay!"

IT SOUNDS LIKE ONE OF YOUR CORE FAMILY VALUES IS INTENTIONALITY.

MATT: It certainly hasn't been perfect, but we do try to be intentional to make sure those important conversations happen. Car rides are also one of those great times to talk. We were in the car for an hour and a half each way yesterday on a family trip, so there were intentional times to talk because they couldn't leave!

DEBBIE: Sometimes, parents can feel like they aren't doing enough. I feel like that's something we all have to overcome in parenthood—*I should be doing more. That was too much*—and you need to have a peace on the inside that you are doing the best you know how and you are learning a lot on the way. I say that regularly to my kids: "I want you to know that I am doing the very best job that I know how. It's not perfect." I have regularly apologized to my kids. I think that's a lot of times something parents don't do—just saying, "I was in a bad mood…that was nothing about you. I'm sorry." That is a regular part of our life, and that is so freeing to me—to be able to think, *You know what, just go in there and apologize*…and then you let it go.

WHAT DOES IT LOOK LIKE FOR YOU TO PARTNER WITH THE HOLY SPIRIT IN RAISING YOUR SONS? CAN YOU GIVE US A SPECIFIC EXAMPLE OF HOW THE LORD HELPED YOU IN A TOUGH MOMENT?

MATT: For us, partnership is asking the Holy Spirit, "Will you help me? Will you help me with this moment? Will you help me with this child? Will you help me with this situation? Give us wisdom." We ask for that a lot, because we don't inherently have the answers. I think just asking Him and trusting. In James 1:5, He said if we ask He'll give us as much wisdom as we need. As our sons get older it seems like situations are more complex than they used to be. I can think of this one tough situation.

One of our sons had a girlfriend, and it was an unhealthy relationship. We coached him as best as we could to get out of that relationship, but it just kept getting more and more unhealthy. So, we were asking the Lord a lot. We did everything we could, but it was not changing. And finally, I just felt the Lord say, "Then you've got to end it." Now I tried to coach him to make good decisions himself, but this wasn't happening and he was still in our household.

So, I said, "As of this day, you no longer have a girlfriend." That's not how I would have told someone else to parent, to be honest! But, at that point, we felt like we had to step in, because it was really unhealthy. I said, "No more girlfriend from this date on. You can blame me, I don't care." So he broke up with her, and it got a little bit crazy after that from her side; it was a super controlling situation. But within a week I'd say, we felt like our son came back to life. He completely changed on the inside—he was free. Stepping in in that way was super uncomfortable, but I feel like the Holy Spirit led us to do that in that moment. Again, that's not what I would've necessarily taught to someone, but you know, Jesus didn't say the same thing twice to the same person as far as advice. That's part of why we have the Holy Spirit, because each situation is going to be a little unique, and we do need Him.

IF YOU COULD SHARE A WORD OF ENCOURAGEMENT TO PARENTS READING THIS, WHAT WOULD YOU SAY?

MATT: I would say the Spirit of Truth and the Guide of Life lives on the inside of us. If we will ask Him in any and every situation what to do, instead of trying to find a formula or something that's even worked for someone else that could be a good thing, He will reveal help as we do our best to lead and guide our kids. I believe that, as a parent, God gives you the gift of being able to have the wisdom you need to parent. Lean into Him for those things.

DEBBIE: Remember that your voice is a creator; your words are a creator. The way you speak to your child is creating something, and so you want to always come from the perspective of life. You can speak life while you're correcting. When you're speaking about your child to other people, speak from the perspective of life. Speak life!

MATT: One more thing I'd say is to highlight incentives for your kids. As an example, with one of our kids, early on he wouldn't quit sucking his thumb. He was four years old and he was still sucking his thumb. We tried a lot of different things to try to get him to stop that. Nothing was working. The Lord gave me the thought to give him an incentive. So I said, "I'll give you a dollar if you won't suck your thumb today." And with that incentive—being for something rather than just against something—he didn't suck his thumb all day! He wanted that dollar. The next day I did the same thing. And he didn't suck his thumb the next day. It cost two dollars for him to stop sucking his thumb. After being frustrated beforehand, we realized that Jesus is really that way. It's not about what He's against or that we're living against all the evil in the world. It's what we're for—it's the Kingdom of Heaven! It's life, it's joy, it's peace. It's touching other people's lives, being filled with His Spirit and being close to Him in our walk with Him, rather than, "Don't do this, don't do this, don't do this." As parents, we can incorporate being for things, not against them.

YOU CAN DO IT

Recipe for Being Encouraged by the Father ——— Sean Feucht

Quite often these days, as my children grow, I feel like I am teaching them less and less and learning more and more from them. The role reversal as a parent is miraculous and beautiful if you fully embrace it, "for unless you change and become like little children you will never enter the kingdom of God" (Matthew 18:3, NIV). Recently, we took advantage of a seventy-one degree January day by loading up the kids' bikes to cruise our normal route through our country neighborhood. My son, Malachi Christopher (we call him "Kai"), was so frustrated that he couldn't ride his bike on the dirt path like his older sister, because his training wheels kept getting stuck in the mud. This eventually pushed him over the edge to want to learn how to ride his bike "like a big boy" without training wheels.

Kai is by far our most cautious, tender child, and we have been working specifically on not allowing the "middle child" stigma to settle on him. Kate and I both know that this is not his portion. This moment was an open door to help him conquer his fears, so I leapt at it! Meanwhile, Kate was playing "safety mom"—which has probably saved Kai's life a few times already—encouraging me not to fling Kai down the biggest hill in our neighborhood. We agreed on a location and went for it. After a few times of him falling pretty hard and scraping his arms and legs, I held him in my arms and whispered into his ear while he was sobbing, "You can do it, Kai! You were made for this!" Still crying, he agreed to give it one last try. I began pushing Kai, his legs peddling

faster than ever before; he started to whisper to himself, "I can do it, I can do it, I can do it," until it was loud, bold and echoing through the air around us. Even though his little arms were shaking and he was gritting his teeth in panic, his heart was steadfast. As I gave him a last push at the end of the driveway onto the hill, I could feel the Father like never before. He reminded me I had been here before many times—it was me who was on the bike. Through that moment of risk, trust and letting go with my own son, the Holy Spirit was reminding me of my own journey in life. There've been so many times I've felt unsure or afraid, but the Father surrounded me with, "You can do it, Sean!" Kai conquered his fear that day and rode his bike in a complete circle before softly crashing in the dirt. We exploded as a family around him, hugging him and telling him how amazing and bold he was. I could almost hear Heaven doing the same thing in response. It was one of the most powerful moments I've ever had with my firstborn son. Some of our greatest frustrations can lead to our biggest breakthroughs in life, if only we'd hear the Father whisper, "You can do it."

Prompt: Have you ever felt utterly defeated? Remember back to that moment of despair, but imagine the Father holding you in His strong arms while you wept. Listen now for His voice that whispers, "You can do it! I believe in you." Let the encouragement of the Father fill you with bravery and confidence. Ask Him, "Lord, what word of encouragement do you have for me in this moment of feeling defeated?" Journal His voice.

THE GLAD GAME

Recipe for Teaching Your Children the Value of Gratitude ——— Sarah Roach

Artwork ——— Justina Stevens

"Enter His gates with thanksgiving…" (Psalm 100:4, NIV).

My two kids are best friends, champions of each other's hearts. But as deep as their love runs, like all siblings, they have moments of strife. Several years ago after a disagreement (a toy-grabbing, tear-producing, meltdown-evoking scuffle), I sent them to their rooms and sat by myself with Jesus for a minute. The last thing I wanted was to stand them face to face and require a forced "I'm sorry," uttered with scowls still lingering on their faces. I didn't want to brush past the issue by coercing them to repeat meaningless words; I wanted to tackle this issue from the heart.

A word dropped into my heart: gratefulness. The Lord said to me, "They need to remember what they are thankful for about each other." *Really, Lord? Will this work on a three- and six-year-old?* I was doubtful they could see past their frustration in the moment, but I had a suspicion that God wanted to show all of us something valuable. I told them both that they had to sit quietly in their rooms and ask the Father to show them three things they were thankful for about the other person. I sat in the hallway between their rooms wondering how long it would take. In two minutes, Evie burst out of her room, her countenance totally changed. "I am thankful that Brighton builds forts with me and plays games with me. I am thankful that he is kind to me and that he makes me laugh. I love that he is my brother and that he helps me find things when I lose them," she said buoyantly.

I watched Brighton's sweet, three-year-old face soften and give in to the love that was being offered by his big sister. Evie's list continued, and before she could even finish getting her words out, Brighton, who couldn't contain it any longer, burst out with his own lengthy list: "I'm thankful that she shares! She lets me sleep in her bed. She gave me a jelly bean yesterday…" They grabbed each other up and hugged like they had been reunited after years of separation.

In that seemingly ordinary moment, we all witnessed a beautiful truth play out before our very eyes. A quiet moment away with the Lord and hearts willing to see with His eyes transformed enemies into friends in a matter of minutes. Psalm 100:4 says that we "enter his gates with thanksgiving." When we turn our hearts from anger, frustration and fear toward thankfulness, we enter into an entirely new world. We see challenges differently, and we see people differently. That morning we witnessed the miraculous shift that happens when we open our hearts to thankfulness and let it overflow the banks of our hearts. Gratitude is not a command, a forced exercise; it's not words choked out of rigid hearts offered up to do their religious duty. Gratitude is a gift we can open with the help of the Holy Spirit. It unlocks secrets, hidden joys and mysteries that aren't accessible with a hardened heart. It's an invitation to enter His Kingdom and walk into the fullness of the beauty of the life He has for us.

Thankfulness has the power to change people, relationships, families, cities. Evie and I watched the Disney movie *Pollyanna* when she was younger, and it made an impression on both of us. In the movie, Pollyanna shared with people in a town cloaked in sadness, depression, greed and religion that when she felt sad, when she felt lack, when she felt angry, she played the Glad Game. She would stop in the middle of her tracks and think of things right there to be glad about. There was always *something* to be thankful for. As simple as this sounds, it is revolutionary. Pollyanna created her own beautiful world of thankfulness in the midst of that tired, depressed, hopeless town. Her world of thankfulness eventually began to breach the banks of her own life and spill into the hearts and lives of the townspeople until, at the end of the movie, they put up a sign declaring the city "The Glad Town."

Our family plays the Glad Game frequently. My kids often remind me to step aside and enter the gates of thanksgiving to be transported into His presence, His goodness. When stress builds up and papers get lost, dogs chew valuables, vacuum cleaners explode dust all over newly cleaned floors and I head toward a grown-up meltdown, Evie will calmly walk over and throw her arms around my neck and say, "This is frustrating, Mommy, but think of all the good things in our lives." Gratefulness changes everything. Thankfulness bathes our eyes to see the way He sees. All it takes is one little turn, and limitations give birth to creative inventions, problems become adventures and enemies become friends.

Prompt: Ask the Holy Spirit to bathe the eyes of your heart to see in a new way. Ask the Lord to lead you through the doors of thanksgiving as you write down everything that comes to mind that you can thank Him for: life, breath, family, safety. Be specific. Don't stop when you think you're finished. There's always more. Press in deeper, and keep writing. Ask Him how you can be a conduit of thankfulness in your home to change the atmosphere. Journal His response. Ask the Lord to help cultivate gratitude in your heart, so that in every situation you usher yourself and those around you into His presence with thanksgiving.

Honest & Open

An Interview on Relating to Your Children with Martin & Anna Smith

By Allie Sampson & Erin Gravitt / Photography from Personal Collection

Erin opens the door and I step into her cozy kitchen. Taking my shoes off, my heart beats a little faster. I am full of joy and anticipation, not quite sure what to expect. Erin and I look at each other and get caught up in a wind of laughter. "Can you believe this?" she smiles, "We get to interview Martin and Anna Smith." I can hardly believe it. I remember the sound of Martin's voice on the other side of my childhood boombox, laying confident anthems and prayers before the Lord. I remember singing the songs he wrote in my mother's minivan and from the blue chairs that lined our sanctuary. I remember feeling Heaven tangling fingers with Earth as Delirious? lyrics rang truth into my heart. I remember the sensation of returning home.

Today I'll hear that voice again, alongside his stunning bride. Martin and Anna Smith are vivacious, colorful people whose lives are marked by love and joy in the deep places. They live in Brighton, England with their six children. They are some of the most sincere people I've met, and their love for marriage, family and vulnerability is overwhelmingly tangible. We met with them to hear more about their heart for family and building a culture of honesty. As you read their thoughts, may you be refreshed and inspired to give your heart fully to the relationships that matter most.

CAN YOU TELL US A BIT ABOUT HOW YOU MET AND FELL IN LOVE?

MARTIN: I first met Anna when she was sixteen years old. I was a sound engineer at a recording studio, and Anna came in as part of a choir. I thought, *Oh wow! She looks pretty hot!* It wasn't until maybe a year later that I actually spoke to her.

ANNA: Martin sang at my eldest sister's wedding. When I saw him I thought, *Oh, he's quite interesting!* And then when I heard him sing I thought, *Oh yeah, I could get to know him. That could be fun!* But I just remember him wearing the most appalling suit that day—he had a suit that was three sizes too big. I thought, *Nice voice. Shame about the suit.* Martin was the first person I dated, and I was twenty when we married. It'll be twenty-four years married next July.

TELL US ABOUT YOUR CHILDREN.

ANNA: There's Elle-Anna, who is twenty and just beautiful. She just got married. She's very easygoing and fun to be with—a very kind big sister. Then we've got Noah, who is eighteen. He's a youth and worship intern in Birmingham. It's been really hard because he left home this past September. I really miss him so much. He loves people, children, loves drumming, loves worship. He fills a room. Indi-Anna is next. She's seventeen and lots of fun. She's at college. She's very strong-natured and absolutely stunning. Then we've got Levi who is fifteen. He checks to make sure I'm okay every day. He's the one who looks after me when Martin's away. Then we have Ruby-Anna who is twelve. She is my crazy one who is most like Martin. She dances and sings constantly—just quite unaware of the norms of her age. Everybody adores her. Mary, the last one, is ten. She is a go-getter. She's very competitive, very strong, very intelligent and plays soccer for our city team.

All of them love Jesus and have found their own relationship in their own different ways; we talk about it around the table—it's a very open conversation. We talk about why we believe, if we believe, who is struggling with believing, what if He's not there? What if God isn't real? Those are the things we talk about, and when I say, "talk around the table," it's never just our family. It's whoever is there. I mean, there are five or six other people who have just come over for dinner right this second. They're just boys and girls from all over who just hang out here. Around our table we talk about absolutely everything. There's nothing that we don't talk about.

MARTIN: That's one thing I've had to get used to with Anna—she just has a total open house policy. It is amazing; we never know from day to day who is going to be here.

SO, FOUR OF YOUR KIDS ARE TEENAGERS RIGHT NOW. WHAT IS THAT LIKE?

ANNA: Yes, we have four teenagers at the minute and I absolutely love it. People say, "Watch out for those teenage years," but I love this season. I think teenagers are fantastic—they'll tell you what they think, and they all disagree. Everyone has a different opinion; everyone's got a reason why they have a different opinion. I love it. I sit there at the table and I listen to it all because they are passionate. And they're intelligent—this generation is intelligent! These teenagers, they've read their stuff. You can't use simple answers for these guys. They are ready, and they've got some things to say. They're going to change the world, and I'm not just talking about my own children. I love the honesty. I love their view of church. I love their view of how they want church to look, of how society is. I love what they talk about. I love that they love the presence of God.

MARTIN: Authenticity is the key with teenagers—and it's the grace of God, isn't it? If there's any way that we're different outside of the house than we are inside the house—oh, they will smell it. They hate it. Kids hate it, don't they? Our kids will tell us all the time, "Oh Dad, why did you do that? You didn't speak to that person very well." If there's any of that super-spirituality within the culture of your life, that's going to explode at some point. And if you're pretending to be something that you're not, you need to give it up now. It's not going to work. Teenagers will expose that. No matter your behavior as a parent, your kids will learn that behavior and then they end up just doing the same.

WHAT ARE THE CORE PILLARS THAT HAVE SHAPED YOUR FAMILY AND MARKED YOUR YEARS AS PARENTS?

ANNA: Honesty. I think just being really honest about stuff—definitely thinking about others before yourself. Don't do to others what you wouldn't do to yourself—those common pillars that Jesus talked about. I was brought up as a pastor's kid in a different era—there are things that we talk about now that were quite taboo that I never got to talk about around the table. I think in the next generation what's really important is authenticity and just speaking about what's going on in your head. I always want my children, and whoever is around my table, to have the freedom to ask what they want about anything. I think that's really, really important. It's also important to me that each and every one of them finds God in their own way, not just 'believing' because they've been brought up in a Christian family—not just because we go to church. I want them to find their own connection with God—that to me is the most important thing. Whatever age they are, I want them to feel like there's never any question that they can't ask us.

MARTIN: I'd say openness. We've always really encouraged "there's nothing that's off the table." There's nothing that's out of bounds. Just talk about anything, even if they feel like it's going to hurt us. Let's at least have an environment where we can discuss it. I like that they listen to crazy music because it gives us a chance to talk about the stuff that they're into and what their friends are into. I'd rather be involved in it; I'd rather them play me something in the car that they're into rather than me not know about it. And I think if you keep it all above board, all honest and open, somehow then the rebellion thing doesn't get a look in—because what do they rebel from? We try to create a culture where they can bring all their friends in and have an open environment rather than feel judged. Judgment and that sense of "not quite good enough" is not great for family. Of course I've made many mistakes in this process and no plan is perfect but learning to say sorry to your kids is part of the journey!

WHAT'S ONE RHYTHM THAT YOU'VE SET AS PARENTS AND HOW HAS IT SERVED YOUR FAMILY?

MARTIN: One thing that's been really important to us over the years is holidays and vacations. We've always been a really big vacation family. I think that principle applies—it's not about how much money you earn or going to fancy places—that's all relative to who you are. But I think it's the commitment: every year we are going to abandon everything at home. It's just us and the kids.

ANNA: When our house is so full of people all the time and Martin's away, it's really sacred for the kids to have that time just with us. No interruptions. No emails. No phones. No anything. It's just us. Last year was the most incredible time where the kids opened up about stuff and talked about some of their feelings. It was incredible. Very, very healing. Very emotional. Very real. It was definitely worthwhile.

YOU'VE TALKED A LOT ABOUT MAKING A SAFE PLACE FOR YOUR KIDS TO BE OPEN WITH YOU. HOW DO YOU NAVIGATE BEING VULNERABLE WITH YOUR CHILDREN?

MARTIN: I'd say the big stereotype in the previous generation—our parents' generation—would be that lack of connectivity—no emotional connectedness. So, our generation grew up thinking that you didn't get involved with your kids, that it was all about discipline, that the mother-father roles were very separate, that parents shouldn't show emotion. Parents would never allow their children to see an argument or a disagreement—you just kept that sort of front: we are the parents and you are the children. But I think that's changing a little bit. We haven't done everything right, but I think that we've tried to model to our kids that we aren't perfect and we've got our own stuff that we're figuring out.

Of course, there are certain things that are private that Anna and I only talk about when we're on our own, but I do think there are things you can bring your children into and let them discover early on that life and relationships are complicated. There's conflict.

ANNA: If we do have conflict in front of the children—which of course we do—we teach them how to make up, how to apologize. We make sure that they see how we resolve our arguments. So again, it's all about being honest with each other. Sometimes we'll get in a disagreement and one of the children will say, "Well Dad, you really didn't listen to Mom the other day," because they feel free to totally say anything to us. They'll say, "Come on, Dad," or, "Dad, you're not getting it." The same thing to me, "Mom, you're not being very kind to Dad. You're being a bit harsh with him." I love it, because I listen to them and I say, "Yeah, you're right. I am being harsh and I'm sorry." I think it's really important to teach your children from a young age how to cope when you don't agree on the same things and how to navigate through that, and how to work it out with their siblings as well.

WHAT WISDOM CAN YOU SHARE ABOUT HOW TO BUILD TRUSTING RELATIONSHIPS, SPECIFICALLY WHEN KIDS ARE IN THEIR TEENAGE YEARS?

ANNA: Just spend time with them. Just listen to them, give them time. You know, Noah, my eighteen-year-old, is super grumpy in the mornings. He never speaks to anyone in the mornings—he just doesn't. But do you know what, if you stay up until midnight and he comes back from something, he will talk and talk and talk. And it's absolutely beautiful. It's just that it's at midnight, and that's not totally the right time for me, but I get the best out of him then. It's about sacrificing in that moment—I love him, I want to hear him, I want to hear what he's got to say and what he feels, in his time, not in my time. Not when it suits me. Not when it actually fits in with my life. This is about handing over my time.

With Indi, do you know what she really loves? She loves me to take her to school, and in that time I have with her in the car, I get to chat with her. She thinks it's me taking her there, but really I'm loving just hanging out with her. With each one of our kids we're just grabbing those moments—especially as teenagers, because they go off and they're busy and they've got their friends. It's not about them fitting in with us—it's about finding those moments to be present with them. It's not about giving them rules about what they should or shouldn't be doing. It's actually about having fun and asking them how they're doing and what's going on in life. Just being super normal. And I'm not their friend—I don't want to be one of their mates. I'm Mom, and I love being their mom. I find being their mom such a privilege. I've been entrusted with these beautiful kids, and God's given me everything I need so they can become everything that He wants them to be, and I find that absolutely miraculous—that He's entrusted me with everything. So, I feel like, *Okay God, I'm going to do the absolute best I can in the time I've got with them. Help me do it well. Help me do this season well. Help me know what to say and when to say and when not to say something.* Parenting is about asking God for wisdom and listening to His timing.

children remind us there are rooms

Poem ———— Stephen Roach

Children remind us there are rooms in our hearts
we never knew were there.
Like recurring dreams of childhood homes,
we discover interior landscapes
our natural eyes never witnessed.

Alcoves and corridors appear
where once were only walls.
Familiar grounds
take on new shapes.

Children call us again to curiosity,
never believing the edge of the cliff
is the edge of our abilities.
They call us back to the kingdom
we have failed to see
amidst our towering cities
of paychecks and appointments.

Children are a timeless race
whose days and hours smash shapeless
into eternity—
an eternity of play, of make-believe,
which suspends our adulthood disbelief
and makes us believe.

We are meant to be
the heroes,
the queens,
the giant slayers,
tiny beings who possess the ability to fly
straight off the cliff,
where enemies plummet to the dust below.

Children keep us from crowning king
the stalemate of daily ritual
and give meaning to our expanding hearts,
an exhilarated pulse
beyond the thud of our own gratifications.

Children teach us the world
is not fixed as we imagined
but pliable, able to be shaped
by faith and wonder.

Broken branches become swords,
bedsheets become shelters
set up in pathless forests.
We can only enter
when we leave our wallets, watches, keys
by the entrance
and crawl on our knees into an illuminated world
we were ever meant to inhabit.

Theirs is a kingdom of curiosity, of endless discovery,
smashed shapeless into eternity.

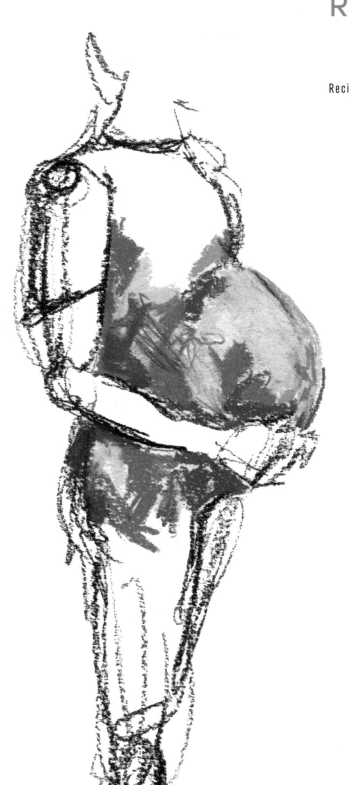

RECEIVE RATHER THAN RESIST

Recipe for Laying Down Your Life in Family ——— Rachel Upton

Artwork ——— Justina Stevens

Jason and I married in our very early twenties, while still students at university. As spouses, we had the great gift of spending every part of every day together, as we were in all the same classes. From undergrad we went straight into graduate school and completed our Masters of Divinity programs together. I was competing horses at the time, and Jason would come to every competition to cheer me on. He held the honored role of stall cleaner and groom. Ministry was also always done together. We were partners in everything and had a front row seat and very active role in helping each other grow. There were some minor bumps in the road early on in learning how to communicate and how to be a team in all things, but those years were marked by lots of fun, lots of learning and lots of wild worship nights in our apartment and in several churches with friends. There was very little "laying down my life" or losing myself in this season. Nothing really had to die in me; life was easy. We even had enough time and energy to get a puppy by the end of graduate school. After we completed our higher education, we decided that we were ready to become parents. Who is ever "ready" to become parents?! Parenting is on-the-job training at its finest. There are a few readying principles, but the real skills are only learned through actually parenting in real time. After five years of marriage, we had our first child, Samuel.

Two weeks after Samuel was born, Jason left for Nashville on a tour bus to lead worship, minister and finish recording his *Faith* record. I was left at home with this new, beautiful baby boy who was up all night. Samuel projectile vomited several times a day. It was extreme! Being new parents, we were both very worried that something was seriously wrong. Because of this, it seemed impossible for me to travel. So, I chose to stay home. A lot of changes seemed to take place all at once. Jason and I were no longer spending every day together. Most painful of all, we no longer had endless hours each day to pray and connect with the Lord. I had no public outlet for doing ministry, which I had trained and dreamed about doing for many years. I definitely went through an identity crisis. *Who am I now? Am I still a minister, still a prayer warrior, still a student of the Word? Are my husband and I still a team if he is traveling and I'm at home?* I felt like the rug of my life had just been pulled out from under me. The life I'd imagined where a baby would fit in seamlessly was not reality. I felt as if I was losing myself. Parenting required a whole new level of sacrifice and work that I wasn't prepared for. I *loved* this baby. In fact, I was obsessed with him. Yet, somehow I had missed the memo that this adorable little life would severely shake up my whole world. Eventually, we adjusted. We figured out Samuel's health issues and I was able to begin traveling on half of the ministry dates with Jason. We were all together again—now with Samuel strapped to me or laying on the stage next to us. Life seemed meaningful to me again. I was, once again, involved in ministry. Most importantly, I was out of the house! All of this made me feel a bit more alive.

Less than two years later our second child, Emma, was born. Just as we started getting our bearings with one baby, she shook things up again. She also never slept at night. This threw a new curve ball into our plan to travel and minister together. I tried in the beginning to travel with both babies, but being up all night, ministering all day and parenting in-between soon took a toll on me physically. This time I happily chose to stay home. I needed some stable ground beneath me. Again, it would mean that Jason and I would be separated a bit more, which was hard for us. Jason loved to travel and minister, but it was torturous for him to leave me and the kids. He hated missing out on moments at home as much as I hated missing out on moments with him. I felt as if I was being left behind. I hardly had any time to connect with Jason, much less, the Lord. It was a very lonely season for me.

In the early years of being a new mom, the Lord gave me a game-changing thought while on a silent retreat: "I can keep resisting and dreading this calling of motherhood and be miserable, or I can fully jump into it, become great at it and be grateful." Since then, my circumstances haven't changed, but my attitude drastically has. I began to shift my mindset from "survival mode" to "fully living the life I've been given mode." I finally chose to jump fully into my calling of being a mom. The Ministry of Motherhood became a gift to be received rather than resisted. I felt a new grace and joy in the daily tasks and needs of my family. Serving my family was

hard work, but it was no longer a crushing burden. I was now very much aware that being Mom was both a great calling and the most important ministry I could ever do. Motherhood does not just *happen* to women; it is a calling one must choose to accept and enter into with resolve and joy.

Motherhood is a life of prayer and study. I no longer felt shame about not having enough "quiet" time to give to the Lord amidst the busy schedule of parenting; Jesus was meeting me in the prayerful discipline of Motherhood! He meets mothers in simple daily tasks. Motherhood is a choice impossible to make without first having chosen to enter into a life of prayer with Jesus. It is the greatest School of Prayer one can ever attend. Marriage is a sacrament entered into by two people who make a commitment before God and man to participate in the ongoing creation of the other. Like marriage, parenting is all about receiving *and* becoming. "Laying our lives down," sounds terrifying but Jesus says that those who lose their lives will find it (see Matthew 16:25). The way of Jesus is more about *letting go* and *taking hold of* than it is just *losing*. We let go of our false selves in order to take hold of our true selves. The only problem is that we most often don't know who that true self is. We have to allow ourselves to get a little lost, in order to be truly found. God is a dreamer, and the dreams He has for each one of us are way beyond our wildest imagination. Committing your life to marriage and raising kids will cost you everything—literally! Like me, you may initially feel that you are losing yourself in the process. However, if you jump in fully, you will find your more authentic self, your true self. After twenty-two years of marriage and seventeen years of parenting I am still on this journey of "becoming." I feel confident I will fully embrace every new season as well as I have embraced this season of parenting. One of the greatest gifts is to say that I have very few regrets, because I know I chose to be present.

Prompt: The important question is not how much of our lives we are losing, but rather how much of our lives we will never find if we don't fully engage with the callings we have been given. Take time to ask yourself: *What am I becoming by doing what I am doing? Am I at risk of damaging my own humanity in an effort to be successful at something that is elusive and possibly not even something I am called by God to be doing? Lastly, what are those things that I know for sure I am called to?* Write them down and then begin to make a plan for giving the majority of your time and energy to those things that God is calling you to. What you will find in doing this is that God is always calling us to tasks for the purpose of shaping and forming us into the humans we were always created to be.

ALL THE MARROW OF LIFE

Recipe for Parenting from Passion ———— *Sean & Kate Feucht*

Photography ———— *Personal Collection*

"I did not wish to live what was not life, living is so dear; ...I wanted to live deep and suck out all the marrow of life..."
-Henry David Thoreau, Walden₄

We were the All-American couple—high school sweethearts in Virginia immersed in football and church. Sean owned a real estate company alongside a few other businesses. We were going to make a lot of money and we were going to live the American dream, but God had other, much better plans in mind. Now we travel to unreached, dark, rough places around the world with our three children and consider it a joy to see the presence of God show up through our ministry, Burn 24/7. As a family whose DNA is missions, the Holy Spirit has helped us from the beginning of our marriage to look at our life through seasons; this outlook helps us hold on to hope in parenting and adjusting our perspectives to see the way God sees.

It's been a gift that we can take our children to places all around the world through Burn 24/7— South Africa, Australia, Japan. We love bringing them into different cultures. We were in Jakarta, Indonesia recently, where the Islam call to prayer is broadcast on the intercom systems over the city five times a day. Our kids would hear it and just start dancing and worshiping the Lord; they didn't get serious or think it was evil. They live in simplicity. It's a reminder that we don't have to live under heaviness depending on the spiritual atmosphere of a city—everything can be redeemed. Our kids live that way—it's fascinating to us. We need their perspective to see how God sees.

Last year our family went to minister at a refugee camp in Iraq, and we were nervous that we were going to expose our kids to too much—that they'd lose their innocence. We didn't want them to pick up the weight of this intense situation—war, death, violence, poverty—going on in the world. We explained it to them in a way they could understand, but our six-year-old daughter Keturah really understood. She recognized these refugees were people who had their homes taken away, people who had lost their moms and dads. She was so compassionate toward them and would pray for them and their needs. Amazingly, we saw that she didn't carry around the weight of it. She knew the burden was God's, and that He would take care of

it. Meanwhile, I [Kate] was crying in my room every night carrying the weight of the devastation happening around us. Keturah's response really impacted me.

When you are trying to steward the calling and destiny on your child, there are unique opportunities and challenges in family. With each child we add to our family, we feel the sobriety from the Lord that we are stewarding destinies. Our kids become a product of their environment. We as parents have the ability to create an environment for them to grow, learn and encounter God. Leaning into the Holy Spirit is everything. God has built children with an incredible ability to adapt, and our kids have done just that as we travel the world ministering through worship to different people groups and cultures. We've learned that we shouldn't try to build our lives around our kids; we have built our lives around the calling of God. We believe our kids are going to fit into that perfectly. They don't have a self-absorbed mentality that everything revolves around them. They know they are not at the center of the universe—life is about God, His Kingdom and what we've been called to.

Our three kids have different desires than other kids their age do. We're planning on going back to Iraq on missions in a couple of days to spend Christmas with refugees, and our kids are so pumped about it. They don't care that they'll miss out on holiday stuff, because that's a value we've instilled in them—a heart for people. Every time we travel with them to do ministry, we're planting seeds that they'll always carry in their hearts. Likewise, we get to learn something from our kids, too. This is the beauty of missions and family in our season right now, and our kids are on the journey with us. May we all live deeply and suck all the marrow out of the life that God has given us.

Prompt: Where are you parenting out of fear instead of passion? Invite the Holy Spirit into your next season of parenting. Pray, "Holy Spirit, where are you inviting me into trust as a parent? How can I partner with you to build an environment for my kids to encounter you and grow?" Surrender your fear, and journal His response.

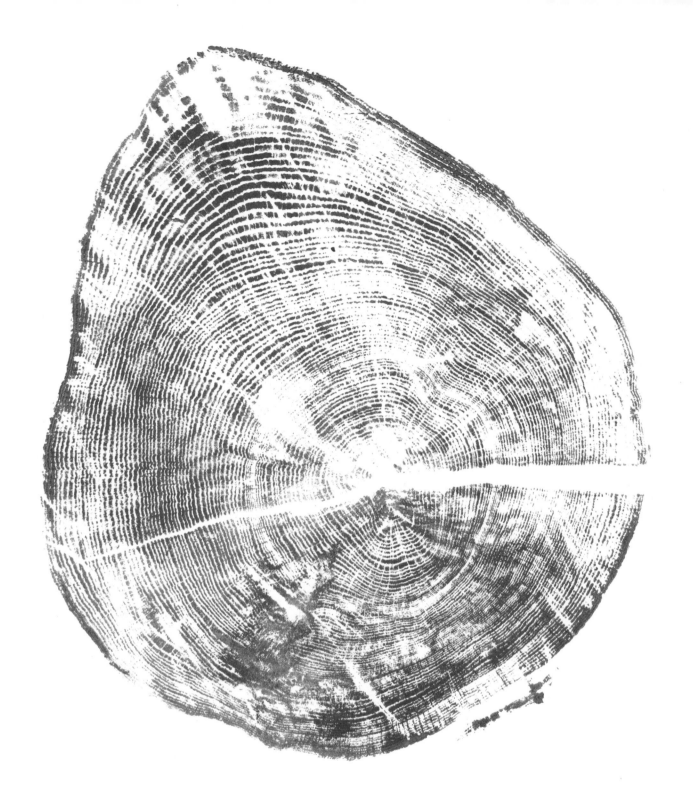

Internal Gaze

Recipe for Obedience ——— Shannon Casteel

Red Oak Woodcut, approx. 72 years old ——— Lindsay Vance & Morgan Campbell

"[Jesus] replied, 'Blessed rather are those who hear the word of God and obey it'" (Luke 11:28, NIV).

I have been a mother for twelve years and in full-time ministry for nine of those years. As my relationship with the Lord has deepened and I've grown to know His character, I've become more aware of His desire to be part of every area of my life. This has taken me time; my first few years of "juggling" ministry and motherhood were tough. Nearly every day I would wrestle through conflicting thoughts: *You haven't done enough. You let your husband down because you were with the kids. You let your kids down because you were doing ministry. You let those you lead down because you were with your family.* Night after night I'd try falling asleep with fresh resolve: *Not tomorrow. No more meetings. I'm taking the kids to the beach for the day. Tomorrow, I'll have a date with my husband. Tomorrow, I'm going to be at every meeting.*

I woke up one morning and asked God to let me feel His pleasure over my life. I went through my day leading a prayer set at our University of the Nations campus in Hawaii, teaching leadership training to our new staff, sitting at tables for discipleship meetings and then going home to be with my one-year-old son. I'll never forget the overwhelming presence of God that washed over me in that moment. I surprisingly felt that God was pleased in me in this simple moment of playing with my son; it was surprising because I had been doing "important things for the Lord" all day and had come home to "just be a mom." The revelation hit me that Jesus is still with me in the simple moments of my life. I didn't leave Him behind at a prayer set or designated worship time. He is "Christ in me" (Galatians 2:20).

Years ago I helped host a women's gathering at the University of Washington. I was standing at the back of the auditorium during worship, looking across a room of 150 young students who were hungry for God. I had recently found out that I was pregnant again with our fifth child, and the reality of the weighty demand on my life suddenly hit me. I confessed to the Lord, "I am totally overwhelmed." He whispered a reply, "No, you're not." With a slight laugh, I responded, "No, no. I am. I am totally overwhelmed." "No, you're not," repeated the Lord. "The enemy has been lying to you for years telling you that you're overwhelmed, but I'm telling you today that you are not overwhelmed."

I thought, *Wait a minute. I've been believing a lie all this time?* I couldn't believe it; I didn't *have* to be overwhelmed! Being a mother, doing ministry and saying yes to various opportunities didn't have to be overwhelming. I suddenly became angry—angry at the enemy and at this lie that had been robbing me of peace and joy for so many years. This lie continually robs mothers all the time. It shouts, "You are a mom who is already too busy and in over your head!" It makes every external circumstance feel like a burden, an added weight rather than a life-giving opportunity. It inflicts guilt, saying, "You aren't a good mom if you do anything

besides raise your kids." It causes mothers to reject additional invitations from the Lord out of fear that "it's just too much." It creates a survival mentality with thoughts like, *I have to spend eighteen years just being a mom, and then I can really do important ministry for God.*

In that moment, I immediately repented and broke that lie off of my mind. The Lord revealed to me that when I say yes to more—whether that's more children, influence or ministry opportunities—He is actually inviting me to "abundant life" (John 10:10). Heidi Baker once said, "God never invites us to less; He always invites us to more." I believe the "more" is obedience. It's being fearless in saying yes to what God is calling us to and rejecting the fear of being overwhelmed. And it's being fearless in saying no to what God isn't calling us to and rejecting the fear of man. What I have seen and experienced is that most women are fearful of "too much," and therefore they do nothing. The women who say yes to everything are often overcompensating. Ultimately, no one seems to be listening and trusting the voice of the Lord to lead them into abundant life. The abundant life is always a loving, obedient "yes" to Jesus (II John 1:6). It's radical obedience to trust and sacrifice, whatever that might look like. It's moving when He says *move* and getting still when He says *rest.*

My spirit's ability to rest isn't determined by external circumstances but by my internal gaze, which is set on Jesus. I have set my affections on Him in all aspects of my life—when I'm with my children, when I'm preaching and when I'm doing dishes. I invite Him into every moment of my life. He loves being with me and my kids, being on my dates with my husband and being in ministry meetings when I get the joy of sharing about Him with others. I'm not waiting for my kids to grow up so I can do what I'm "really" called to do. Compartmentalizing our lives is a ridiculous notion that has enslaved so many to bitterness and disappointment! No matter the time or place, I have set my heart to honor Jesus with my life, my thoughts, my actions and my body. My life in Jesus—free of compartments—is my gift to my children, my husband, to the body of Christ and to a hurting, dying world that is longing to see Him.

Prompt: As followers and lovers of Jesus, we must continuously ask the Lord to give us eyes to see the way He sees. Jesus is not reserved for only one area of our lives. Wake up tomorrow, and engage Him. When you speak, acknowledge in your heart that He is with you. When you spend time at home with your kids, say out loud, "He is with me." Everything in your life can spring from the overflow of your relationship with Jesus. I encourage you today to intentionally set your heart and affections on Him; simple obedience is the gateway to the abundant life we all desire. Invite Him with this simple prayer: "Let me feel your pleasure over my life."

1 Jedidiah Jon
2 Henry Christopher
3 Lewis Bennett
4 Quill Reverie

fresh
eyes

Photography ——— *Personal Collections*

This series is a vulnerable reflection of parenthood from the fresh perspective of eight new mothers and fathers in the Cageless Birds community. May their stories of struggle and triumph in parenting with God give a newfound lens for you to cultivate wonder in the most unlikely of circumstances.

a brand new place

Prompt for Giving In to the Tension of Transition ——— *by Justina Stevens*

I had only been a mother for five days. My husband, Jake, and I were smitten with our beautiful son, Jedidiah. He was perfect, with blue eyes and dark hair, and he slept all the time and barely cried; we felt like champions. After six days of bliss, something changed about our baby—he started crying all the time. Inconsolable crying became our background music. Laying next to me on his belly was the only possible way he would fall asleep, if he slept at all. I was frustrated in the uncharted territory; I wanted to have the answers, but I didn't.

One afternoon in particular, Jedidiah was kicking his arms and legs, squirming in discomfort. I was sitting next to him for an hour patting his back, wishing he would fall asleep just for a little bit. I remember taking a deep breath, trying to keep it together. I exhaled, "I am so tired, Father. I don't know what to do." I felt the presence of the Holy Spirit greet me, as if He had been waiting all afternoon for my honesty:

"You know, this is what I've done for you," He said. Wanting to understand, I asked Him what He meant. "Justina, you've experienced so many seasons of transition, and I know they have been difficult. In this moment I am giving you a picture of yourself and the understanding that in every transition, I have

been next to you, close by and soothing you. Your son is in a brand new place with a body that is learning digestion; he is in transition and learning to accept all that's around him. You would rob your son of the beauty of life and change if you tried to put him back in your womb, back to a place where everything was easier. With every transition of your life, my desire is that you could see why I never rushed in to fix, but I rushed in to comfort. I never want to rob you of the beauty of growth and transition, and I never will. Allow me to redeem your misunderstanding of seasons past."

My eyes were full of tears of understanding. In a difficult moment the Father came to wash my feet. The Father came to strengthen and love me, to calm my discomfort and heal my heart in an imperfect scenario. I will treasure that moment my whole life long.

Prompt: It is so easy to try to rush through life's difficulties. More often than not, our moments of growth and understanding are in the tension. In your moments of tension with your children today, take a deep breath and practice honesty with the Father and let Him talk to you. Don't try to hide in your tension. He wants to meet you in your untidy, exhausted places with help and language where you need it most.

the grace of experience

Prompt for Acknowledging Your Neediness ——— *by Jake Stevens*

Becoming a father to Jedidiah Jon is one of the most incredible things I've ever done. It's dramatically expanding and challenging the way I see God. I never had the capacity to understand how He could keep forgiving, keep coming, keep helping and keep answering with kindness until I became a father to Jed. In this season I find that I'm *compelled*, not *repelled*, by Jed's needs.

Recently, my wife Justina and I started feeding Jed things like avocado, banana and squash. He has this habit when I feed him where he'll take one bite and before he can even swallow it, he'll start crying for another one. It's hysterical to me. I watch him and laugh, because there's no question whether I'm going to feed him. He doesn't know that, but I do. He becomes overwhelmed by the need to feel full and gets upset before he's finished what I've just given him. When Jed gets angry and starts crying, it's not because something's wrong with him—he's just hungry—but his need isn't as dire as it feels to him.

I've come to realize that I do this with the Lord all the time. It's easy for me to get upset and believe that nothing will change, but there's no question in the Father's mind whether or not He

is going to meet my needs. When I feel like I'm not getting the things that I need—feeling seen, feeling heard—God isn't striving to make something happen for me. He's not worried. He is joyfully laughing, always ready to meet my needs. He wants my needs to be met as much as I do. I feel an awareness of God's position and posture of joy toward my needs as a helpless child. If I, as a human father, can pull myself out of bed to help my son at two in the morning, that leaves me to wonder, *What will God do? How far will He go? What has He already done?* There is an active nature in God's joy toward our circumstances. He isn't passive towards us. Only eight months into parenting, my view of how God responds to His kids when we are needy and tired is changing.

Prompt: Have you found yourself in a situation where you're irritated by your child's non-stop neediness? Do you feel overwhelmed by your own needs? Consider what God the Father may be waiting to offer you if you will embrace this place where you feel deficient. Ask Him to redefine the word "needy" for you and journal what He says. This week, read His new definition every morning before you start your day. Practice receiving His grace.

every morning

Prompt for Wonder — *by Chris Miller*

Before our son, Henry, was born, my wife Jessie and I would often devote hours in the quiet of a weekend to journaling, creating or reading with coffee in hand. When Henry arrived, our rhythms shifted. Our tendency to lean heavy into spontaneity was challenged as the in-between time took on new meaning. Gone were the casual weekends of sleeping in and extended evenings. I remember feeling completely delirious for the first few weeks back at work. I'd always thought of myself as a night person, but where I would normally push bedtime back, early mornings came to confront me and shake me out of my comfort zone. Our newborn son needed to eat upon waking, have his diaper changed and spend some quality time with us. There was no snooze button in our role as parents. He relied on our presence from the start.

Fatherhood has reintroduced me to the wonder of the morning, beyond the too dark and too early, into the possibility of God's perspective. Most mornings after Henry's first feeding, I take him in my arms and head to the kitchen. He has a little seat on the breakfast table where he can watch my morning ritual as we greet the dawn together. His clear blue eyes follow me as I brew fresh coffee, make breakfast and prepare for the workday ahead. He kicks his legs with delight when I take a seat next to him. We make eye contact as I sip hot coffee and talk to him, narrating the morning's activities, reading out loud from the Word. Some mornings we journey out onto the back porch, his eyes open in wonder at the magic and color of nature. I ask him, "What do you see? Do you see the trees? Can you hear the birds?" He smiles, his countenance bright, clasping his tiny hands in delight. He is in awe. As I engage my son and observe the purity in his response, I feel the Father's playful invitation to see as he does. The addition of Henry in my morning routine has only made my mornings that much richer. If I am this delighted to make space for Henry, how much more is the Father delighted to make space for me each morning? The gift of this season is learning how much the Father delights in my simple being.

Prompt: Make time to wake up early and watch the sunrise with the Father. Let Him into your morning routine and pay attention to how much He delights in you—how much He enjoys your simple presence. Make a list of the ways your own children have reawakened wonder and joy in your heart. Fill up on gratitude then ask the Lord this bold question: "Father, how does my presence enrich your morning routine?" Journal His response to you.

a sacrificial, joyful exchange

Prompt for Making a Worthwhile Exchange — *by Jessie Miller*

"Again, the kingdom of Heaven is like a treasure hidden in a field, which a man found and hid; and for joy over it he goes and sells all that he has and buys the field" (Matthew 13:44, NKJV).

Have you ever wondered what the man in this parable may have sold to purchase the field? What was the "all that he had" enabling him to pursue the purchase of his hidden treasure? As a new mother, the sacrificial, yet joyful, exchange in this parable speaks deeply to me. It suggests that sometimes the security and value of one thing is worth giving up for the hope of another. For years a huge part of my identity revolved around being a high school teacher. Releasing love and seeing students succeed fueled my purpose. It was a daily source of security that affirmed I was important, because what I was doing mattered. Yet the longing to become a mother and stay home to care for my children was hidden in my heart. As my husband, Chris, and I dreamed into growing our family, I contemplated the cost of an exchange. Could I give up the security and affirmation that came from my career to pursue this growing hope in my soul to be a stay-at-home mom?

On a beautiful spring morning, our beloved son, Henry, was born. As they laid my treasure on my chest, the joy that ran through my soul was unlike anything I'd ever felt before, and I knew I had my answer. Everyday Jesus invites me to love my choice. He offers me affirmation in the form of the most perfect gummy smile. On challenging days, when I feel like I still have so much to learn and I miss the confidence I felt at work, I breathe in hope and remember that it will grow again. When tempted to dwell on what I "sold," I practice pausing and looking at my son, savoring the gift it is to mother him. I rest in the beauty of the joy that compelled me. I do not pit my career against staying home with Henry. Both were my choice. In fact, one prepared my heart to pursue the other. What I am doing as a mom matters, and my treasure was worth the cost.

Prompt: Are you are you struggling to savor the season you're in because you felt more affirmed or valuable in the past? Where is the Lord inviting you into a sacrificial, yet joyful exchange? Ask Him what He is longing to give you. Open your hands and make a joyful trade.

Justina + Jed, 9 months

Joel, Kateland + Lewis, 7 months

Jessie + Henry, 8 months

grace to learn

Prompt for Asking for Help ———— *by Kateland Case*

"Pride lands you flat on your face; humility prepares you for honor" (Proverbs 29:23, MSG).

Up until my firstborn son's birth I felt confident that I was going to ace motherhood. The intuition I gained through my experience as a nanny, years of babysitting dozens of children and helping raise my two younger siblings assured me I knew what to do. I had motherhood in the bag, or so I thought.

During the exhausting first weeks of being a new mom, I noticed I was becoming frustrated with myself when Lewis wasn't eating or napping when I thought he would. I'd feel ashamed when I didn't know certain things, like how often to bathe him. Things weren't going as well as I had imagined, but I wanted to be seen as a natural, a savant among moms. In my mind, needing help meant exposing the fact that I didn't know everything, which felt humiliating. I thought I could preserve the mask of perfectionism by reading mom blogs online to get information, rather than humbly calling a fellow mom to talk through my struggles. I wasn't only desperate for advice; I also needed connection and affirmation that I was not alone, not the only one hitting walls. But shame and pride were robbing me of that connection. Regardless of all my experience up to that point, I had never been a mom before and didn't fully know what it would require of me.

The Holy Spirit spoke compassionate truth to me in my frustrations. He said, "Kate, it is pride to think that all your experiences would give you a fast track to bypass learning. You need to give yourself grace to learn how to become a mother to your son." Grace to learn was what I needed for my heart. Not asking for help isolated me from learning and connection. I needed the help of the Father and others in this new season of parenthood. Now that I've accepted I don't have to be the "perfect parent" to Lewis, my load feels lighter. I'm living in freedom—no more false pressure! I have space to reach out and lean into the Father for wisdom on how to parent out of grace, not arrogance. Engaging the gift of learning is not always easy for our egos, but it is always worth it.

Prompt: Are you living under the pressure to parent perfectly? Are you trying to prove something to yourself, your spouse, your friends? Invite the Holy Spirit to help you see one area of your parenting where you are isolating until you feel like you have it figured out. Ask Him to help you catch a moment of pressure this week. When you feel Him bring a moment like this to your attention, practice being vulnerable and reach out to a friend to process.

confident decisions

Prompt for Making Powerful Choices ———— *by Joel Case*

When our son Lewis was just a few weeks old, Kateland and I noticed that something was off. He was having a hard time eating and the frustration he was experiencing at feeding time made him not want to eat at all. We took him in for a check up and our pediatrician pointed out that he possibly had tongue-tie and lip-tie—a tighter than usual attachment, one beneath his tongue and one between his upper lip and gums—and it was affecting his ability to eat. I'd never even heard of this condition. It was minor, but if it went untreated, it could've affected his speech later on. Our pediatrician explained our options. There were a lot of things for us to consider and I felt the pressure of making this decision that could drastically affect my son. *What's the right way to do it? Is it going to be safe? I don't want to ruin him.*

A few weeks later we made the hour-long drive with our ten-week-old for a consultation appointment. If the doctor determined he needed a procedure, they'd do it right there on the spot, taking a laser to our newborn son's mouth to cut the ties. We were nervous. The doctor examined Lewis and thought it would be most beneficial for Lewis to have the procedure. Handing over my son to the nurses brought up a lot of emotions. We'd put a lot of thought into our choice, but there was still an invitation to second-guess ourselves.

Were we sure? Was this the right thing? In that moment, I felt God so clearly, empowering me to guard my mind and be steadfast. We weren't alone and He was teaching us to rise to the occasion to make the choices that only we can make for Lewis. I realized right there that I was able to make a clear, confident choice for Lewis because this is how the Father always makes decisions: unwavering, steadfast.

God is not a double-minded or unsure parent. He's not insecure, worrying about what could go wrong. He joyfully makes powerful choices in leading us, even when it's uncomfortable, toward the things that are for our benefit. In every season I'm realizing that my circumstances are always an opportunity to learn more about God's true nature and become more like Him.

Prompt: Have you been parenting out of insecurity? Ask your heart this honest question: "Where have I been viewing God as an insecure parent instead of the confident, clear Father He is?" Take a moment to humble your heart and trade this view in for the truth. Then ask Him, "Father, where do you want to make space for confidence in my parenting? Show me an area where I've been anxious with my children where you want to meet me with confidence and support." Begin practicing confidence in this area.

to-do lists

Prompt for Balancing Productivity and Self-Compassion ——— *by Erin Gravitt*

After non-stop days of chasing my toddler daughter, cleaning up Play-Doh-stuck toys and hearing her endlessly repeat "no," the five-o'clock hour would habitually find me irrationally irritable. Dirty dishes piled high in the sink, spilling over to counter tops, and abandoned alphabet blocks were scattered across floors, a minefield for bare feet. I resembled a frumpy hermit she-crab, dried yogurt crusted into my shirt.

Before I became a mom, I considered myself an ambitious, high-energy woman who quickly accomplished my goals. I felt productive almost all the time, priding myself in my capability to swiftly execute plans. However, a college degree and career couldn't prepare me for the inexhaustible to-do lists of motherhood. Consistently failing to complete the daily to-do lists I set for myself—simple things, like doing laundry, exercising or changing out of my pajamas—forced me to acknowledge that I couldn't maintain my past ideals of productivity. Blaming myself or making excuses for my five-o'clock temper wasn't working in relieving my mental angst.

Instead of continuing to feel upset every afternoon, one day I decided to surrender my idyllic, inaccurate expectations of productivity. Instead of scolding myself for incomplete tasks, I deliberately released the exasperated rage built in my chest by naming it out loud: "Ugh! I'm so annoyed, Lord!" I substituted hurrying to organize the house with admitting my disappointment to myself, my husband (JD) and the Lord. When JD got home from work, I put the blame game behind me and shared, "I just want you to know that I'm feeling really on edge. You don't have to do anything to make it better. I just want to include you." Amazingly, my aggravation dissipated in realizing I had permission to simply own my feelings. The naming of my negative emotions gave me the freedom and relief I needed to accept my worthiness to God as a wife and mom despite the lack of checkmarks on my to-do lists. This strategy of self-compassion and honesty was a peace offering of inclusion for my husband; it was a graceful receipt of God's unconditional love for me.

Now, I still consider myself an aspiring, reach-for-the-stars kind of woman, but I've started practicing releasing the pressure of achieving worthiness from productivity's standards. When I say bedtime prayers with my daughter in the dim light of her room, I tell her that I'm proud of her: "You did great today." She smiles back at me. The Father tells me that He is proud of me no matter what my to-do list looks like, and I smile back at Him.

Prompt: Regardless of what you did or didn't accomplish today, take a deep breath and imagine the Father smiling at you. Receive the affection, affirmation and delight of the Father over your inherent worth by smiling back at Him. Don't be hard on yourself; instead, practice self-compassion by declaring the Father's heart for you: "I am proud of you."

small world

Prompt for Childlikeness ——— *by JD Gravitt*

"Truly I tell you, unless you change and become like little children, you will never enter the kingdom of heaven" (Matthew 18:3, NIV).

I have loved watching my daughter's world start out small, with every new moment adding a ring to the tree trunk of her life. First, there came a smile, then a laugh, and then her first words: "Dada." She quickly became mobile, pulling herself up on coffee tables and exploring our home. Her little feet stood themselves up to walk, and her first unassisted steps were like the sixteen-year-old's first solo drive behind the wheel—a taste of freedom.

Today, we played in the backyard, and I watched in amazement as she found interest in everything from the dirt in the garden to her bubble-blowing toy lawn mower and the leaves on the ground. She had everywhere to be and go. Abruptly, she stopped in the midst of her toddler investigation and said, "Wash dishes?" This is her way of announcing that she's having fun but ready to move on to the next adventure.

I have no idea why something like washing the dishes brings her so much delight, but her fascination with the world around her does make me stop and think, *How does something so mundane create such awe in her small world?* How much of this feeling of surprise mingled with admiration am I missing in my larger world? Her interactions with seemingly unremarkable things cause me to look again, to look deeper. As an adult, my life sometimes feels complicated; it's easy to become numb to the familiar. My daughter's childlikeness is a reminder; it's a refresher for my heart to hold onto hope rooted in the simplicity of the Gospel. The Kingdom of Heaven is hidden in everyday small moments like dirt, bubbles, leaves and dishes, and it's the children who can see it.

Prompt: No matter how old your children are, make a point to join them in their childlikeness today. Get in their world. Ask the Holy Spirit to give you ideas of how to meet them in this place and to empower you to not rush through it. Pay attention to what this stirs up in your heart and let yourself be affected.

Erin, Quill, JD, 2.5 years

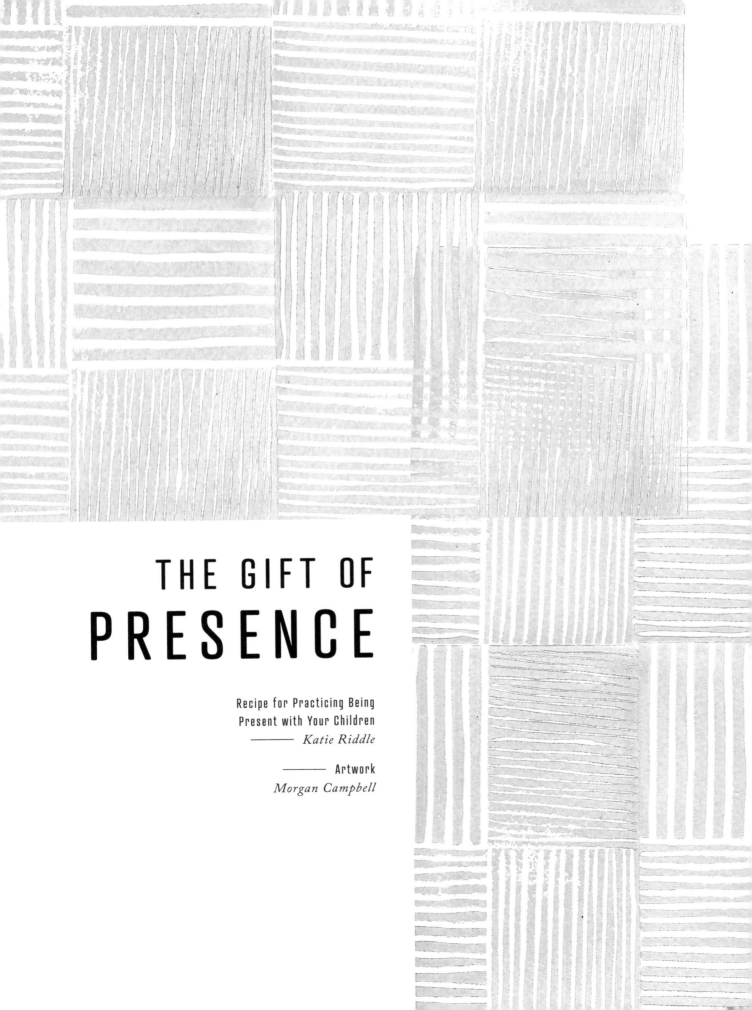

THE GIFT OF
PRESENCE

Recipe for Practicing Being
Present with Your Children
—— *Katie Riddle*

—— Artwork
Morgan Campbell

"If you want to change the world, go home and love your family."
–Mother Teresa

Patience. Self-control. Mindfulness. Endurance. These are the words that generally come to mind when one might think of mothering. But extravagance? How does one mother from extravagance when it can easily be marked by lack? Sleep deprivation from a teething babe, five minutes to clean a house littered with craft supplies before guests arrive and temper tantrums at the end of the day when there's nothing left (outwardly for children and inwardly for adults...most of the time).

Our baby is about to turn six and we just celebrated our eldest's sweet sixteen. I am happy to say that sleep deprivation is rarely a problem and I hope that encourages all the new mothers out there. From my sixteen years of mothering, what I have found to be the most powerful gift we can always extravagantly give to our children is presence. Looking them in the eyes when they speak to us. Making space for conversation, whether driving to the next class or at the table during a meal. Being intentional that when we are together, there is always space for connection.

There is a very unattractive picture that my four-year-old snapped of me two days after giving birth to our fifth child. I'm looking at the camera and have a somewhat blank grin across my face, but was absolutely clueless about what was going on, that Claire even had my phone, and that she took a picture of me. Why would I save such a thing? For starters, whenever I need a good laugh it always delivers, but also to remember to have grace for myself. I knew she was standing in front of me and I had a smile on my face. In this moment, I didn't feel like I had the energy or capacity to be present, but this photo is evidence that I was giving it my best, the fruit of countless moments of choosing to give my daughter my attention. It was as present as I could be in that moment of utter exhaustion.

Presence is a practice. The more we practice, the more effortless it starts to become. Be kind to yourself on the journey as it can still be quite exhausting some days, even when your practice has grown. Sometimes when we have poured ourselves out all day, the gift is a good night's sleep; the drained feeling isn't a sign of failure or that you're not a natural mother, it's because of a job well done and a day of consistent engagement.

Presence is more intimate than proximity and it lavishes time spent together with meaning. It satisfies the primal and truest hunger for human connection that's needed for our children to thrive and gives them the safety and strength to be their truest selves. It says to their hearts, "You are important to me. You are loved and seen. You delight my heart." It is a sacred partnership with our Father in echoing His love for them spoken straight to their wondering hearts. It is the "yes" to their "am I valuable?"

Being present to our children is as different as each child and each stage they're in. Some love eyes locked and listening ears. Others love a good dialogue. Sometimes, for some children, being present is a quiet drive to school while you enjoy their favorite song together, a tender cuddle to begin their day or reading their favorite book for the eighth time before bed. When we are present, we understand the truest connection point for each child in each moment.

Prompt: What are some of the distractions that rob presence from family life that you can remove or make other times for? Be intentional with the in-between times. Ask questions during car drives, make mealtime tech-free, establish a weekly rhythm of one-on-one connection with each child, even if it's only twenty minutes. Ask the Lord what He wants to highlight in them and what you can encourage them in each day. Daily communicate to your children that you see them in simple ways: praise a new achievement, discovery and triumph. Acknowledge when you notice they are struggling or sad and show them you are present enough to be a safe place for them to process. Remember how priceless and nourishing our presence is for the health and development of our children and fully enjoy the utter satisfaction that comes from engaging in each present moment.

SPIRIT-LED PARENT-ING

Recipe for Dependency on the Holy Spirit in Parenting
——— Melissa Helser

Photography
——— Personal Collection

It was a meltdown of epic proportions as we sat in our car at 11:30 at night, Cadence age seven, Haven age four and me. We were waiting for Jonathan to finish packing up his gear after leading worship. It was one of those moments where both children are crying and you are asking yourself, *Why in the world did I keep my kids up this late? This was a terrible decision.* I tried for about forty-five minutes to calm them down, meanwhile getting more and more frustrated at Jonathan. *Where is he?! Doesn't he know I am in here with the kids who are totally exhausted?* Every mom knows exactly what I am talking about…your patience is stretching to its thinnest point, you're breathing heavy and getting louder and louder. Exasperated, I prayed, "God, please help me." Of course it was not a sincere prayer, but a prayer of desperation and total irritation. Immediately I heard the Holy Spirit say, "Ask them where I went." I honestly thought, *What a stupid question, but at this point I will try anything.* I turned around in my seat and said, "Guys, where did the Holy Spirit go? He is the Prince of Peace and I don't think He is in the car." They looked at me, totally confused and through tears said, "We don't know where He went." I replied, "Should we ask Him to come back?" Cadence said, "Yes. I think so." "Holy Spirit, please come back…Yes, Holy Spirit please come back," came out of their mouths through the most pathetic sobbing. Instantly the atmosphere shifted and they went from crying to laughing. I am absolutely not exaggerating; it was so crazy and shocking. They shouted, "He's back, He's back!" As I sat there, totally dumbfounded watching them shift from sobbing to laughing, my first thought was, *Wow, it worked.*

I have asked the Holy Spirit for help in parenting more than any other place in my life. Accessing His profound wisdom has been a life-changing experience for me. I have learned that taking Him at His word and trusting that it is His joy to be my helper gives me the confidence in parenting to fail and succeed with grace and self-compassion. I am not a perfect parent; that was never my goal. My goal has been to walk out the nature of the Father, Son and Holy Spirit, reflecting their kindness, strength, grace, compassion, discipline and love, and then when I fail epically (which is all the time) I have the courage to humble myself and know that my children have to see me make mistakes. Letting our kids see us fail with grace and practice compassion towards ourselves and them is essential to raising kind and strong adults. My kids are much older now and I have countless stories just like that of every age, all of us coming to the end of ourselves and practicing needing the Holy Spirit. The thing is He always comes. Always.

This is what I learned and am still learning: If I take Jesus at His word and believe that He desires to help me and gave me the Holy Spirit for a reason, I never find myself alone in parenting. In the depths, so many parents feel alone and incapable of making the right decision no matter how big or small. The weight of responsibility can feel crushing unless we lean into Him. This is the first thing the Holy Spirit spoke to me when I became a parent: "Melissa, you must teach your children to need my spirit. They will grow beyond their need for you but they will NEVER not need me. Teach them that neediness for me is strength."

The key is PRACTICE. Practice asking Him, practice doing what He says, practice saying you're sorry. Every time I have humbled my heart before my kids and asked the Holy Spirit for help, they have learned that *neediness for Him is strength, not weakness.* It's not enough to just tell them to ask God for help, and then not actually practice ourselves. We must take Him at His word. John 14:15-17 (ISV) says: "If you love me, keep my commandments. I will ask the Father to give you another Helper, to be with you always. He is the Spirit of truth…" Jesus knew we would need a helper. I would say that the gift of the Holy Spirit is the crescendo of the Cross. Jesus swallowed up our loneliness when He decided to come and walk the earth as a human, die the death we could not die and be resurrected to the Father. It was on the Cross that He cancelled the distance and went beyond *God with us* to *God in us.* When we apply that simple truth to every area of our lives we begin to reap the effects of real trust and real practice.

Prompt: Sit down with a pen and paper and brainstorm answers to these questions with the Holy Spirit:

1. *What does it look like to need the Holy Spirit in your parenting?*

2. *What does it look like for you to lean into Him instead of proving to Him that you can do it all on your own?*

3. *What does it look like to let Him help in the simple everyday moments that can suck our energy if we let them?*

4. *What is a simple solution to a normal moment of tension in my parenting?*

Commune with Him in this area of your life that is so important. Practice what He says, and practice the power of letting Him help.

on the
MOUNTAIN RIDGE

Recipe for Connecting with Your Kids through Emotional Care ——— Matt Peterson

Artwork ——— Justina Stevens

Trudging up the mountain ridge in complete darkness, I placed my undersized foot in the indentions in the snow made by my dad as he led the way by flashlight toward our destination. This was the first day of deer season in the Eagle Cap mountains of Eastern Oregon, and I was hoping to get to a high mountain ridge before first light to discover and bag my first big buck. With a rifle strapped over my slight shoulder, I was excited to be with my dad and for the adventure of the hunt. Only minutes into the difficult ascent, asthma attacked. I had struggled with asthma for years and never knew when it would strike. I stopped at the base of a tall fir tree, struggling to inhale oxygen into my lungs, gasping. I hated how it made me feel inadequate and handicapped. I didn't want to be an encumbrance to my dad, but rather a son in whom he was proud. My dad stopped with me, patiently waited and calmly encouraged me, praying until the attack ceased and we were able to continue once again.

Hours later, we were still hunting, making our way around the face of another mountain toward a plateau. My feet were numb from the cold. I wanted to be tough, wanted to endure the cold and the pain while keeping up the pace set by my dad. I waited as long as I could, but the pain was too much. I finally confessed that my feet were hurting and frozen. My dad wasn't angry or even distressed, but instead he sat me down near a grove of trees. He began gathering twigs and small sticks. He swung the pack down from his shoulders, pulled pitch and matches out and built a fire. After the small fire was crackling, he knelt down, removed my boots and began rubbing my frozen feet with his large hands to get the blood flowing once again and warmed them near the flame. We didn't get a buck that day, but I had an experience with my dad that I will never forget. Through this experience, I had a newly formed image of what God, my Father, is like. He is patient, kind and loving, attending to me with His large hands.

Over thirty years after this experience, I now find myself a father of five sons ranging in age from teenagers to their early twenties. Each of my sons is unique with vastly different personalities, hobbies, looks, abilities and needs, and I love them all. One son loves acting and creating, while another loves soccer and lacrosse. While each son has unique needs, they also share common needs, like needing to know and feel that they are strong and have what it takes as men. They all need to know that they are loved, have purpose and have much to give. These are all things that a father can affirm and speak into his children.

Similar to my feelings of inadequacy on that mountain ridge, one of my sons wishes that he had a different physical build, wishes more girls were crazy about him, wishes he didn't have weaknesses that appear glaring and often overwhelm him. He wants to be different. At times he feels woefully inadequate and deeply discouraged, wanting to give up. Life seems easier for everyone else than it does for him, and sometimes he feels like all is against him. During these times, I've learned to stop what I'm doing on my own personal journey and stand with him in the snow, facing the attack with him. I've learned to help him see what is real and give him tools so that he can arrest the thoughts of unworthiness that come against him. I've learned that I can help him identify self-pity when it is at his door so that he can break agreement with it. I've learned to encourage him and be patient with him. I've learned that I, too, can kindle a fire when he feels overwhelmed by the harsh cold world around him so that the blood will flow in his walk once again. As a father, I have the privilege of encouraging and highlighting his great value and reminding him of all that His heavenly Father has ahead for him.

Prompt: Ask God for your eyes to be opened to see Him as He is: patient, loving and kind to us as He leads us through the journey of life. Intentionally get out of agreement with any lie that you are a bother to Him or that He won't stop everything on your behalf. Then, as parents and leaders, let's reflect the nature of our Father to our own children and those following us. Let's allow His patience to operate through us in the midst of others' weaknesses so that we stop what we're doing to stand with them when they get attacked, patiently going out of our way to warm them when the cold of the world attempts to harm their walk. Pray this prayer: "Heavenly Father, help me to see you as you are. Purge my mind and heart from every image and thought of you that is wrong or twisted. Fill me with your nature and love so that I will treat my children and those I lead as you treat and love me. Give me patience, insight and wisdom to speak your words and reveal you to others through the power and comfort of your Spirit."

Through the Fire

An Interview on Revival of Belief through Loss with Blake & Shannon Casteel

By Allie Sampson & Erin Gravitt / Photograph from Personal Collection

Blake and Shannon Casteel are legends. Shannon is Melissa's sister and she and Blake have been dear friends and champions of the Cageless Birds community since the beginning. They are passionate lovers of Jesus and have been involved with Youth With A Mission (YWAM) for the past seven years, leading teams around the world and spreading the Gospel of Jesus. Blake is one of the leaders of Respect the Corners, a functional fitness ministry that trains up coaches as long-term missionaries. Their crew treks Bibles to unreached villages in the Himalayas and uses this avenue to impact their local community. Shannon is on leadership at The University of the Nations and is a public speaker, teaching all over the world at Discipleship Training Schools (DTS) and Brave Love gatherings. Together they raise up missionaries while also raising their five amazing children: Shiloh, Arrow, Brave, Eliana and Mighty.

Blake and Shannon are incredible overcomers. In 2011, right in the heart of their transition into YWAM Kona, they lost their daughter, Selah, full-term. Shannon was thirty-seven weeks pregnant and the devastating loss threatened to take out their marriage, their callings, and ultimately, their faith. In this interview you'll hear about one of their greatest heartbreaks, deepest disappointments and the most powerful, permanent revivals of faith they've ever experienced. Step into their profound belief and vulnerable courage. Set your face like flint and find that God truly is as good as He says He is.

YOU GUYS HAVE A BEAUTIFUL FAMILY AND FIVE AMAZING KIDS. WHAT ARE YOUR FAVORITE THINGS ABOUT YOUR CHILDREN?

BLAKE: As a family, I really love that I never know what I'm going to get, especially around other people. My kids leave me on my toes, and we get into some pretty funny situations. It's challenging, because my sanctification is being worked out through my kids. I didn't know that I could be so easily frustrated or that I was so lacking in patience, but we've grown so much in the Lord through our kids. Our oldest daughter, Shiloh, brings a brutal honesty to our family. She has no fear of man and you will always know exactly what she's thinking. Arrow brings unbelievable wit and laughter to our family. Brave brings such kindness and compassion with his little raspy voice. Eliana brings attitude; she always says what she wants to say. Our youngest child, Mighty, is our little fourteen-month-old joy; she is the one we gather around. No matter how our day goes, we all look at her and see an answered prayer. She's this little baby that we didn't think would make it, but she did! She is a unifying factor in our family.

BEFORE YOU BOTH GOT MARRIED, WHAT DID YOU THINK ABOUT HAVING CHILDREN?

BLAKE: Before we were married, Shannon already had Shiloh. So, even though I didn't know how to raise kids, my mindset

was that I wanted to be a father to this amazing little girl—to show her love, to fight for her. It was a challenge but a very real desire for me. Having more kids was an obvious next step for us. We always prayed and asked the Lord about more kids and we believed what the Lord said in the Bible was true: "Children are a heritage from the Lord, offspring a reward from him" (Psalm 127:3, NIV). We wanted that. We wanted to trust the word of the Lord—that was our outlook. As we had more kids, everything got more awesome and more difficult.

CAN YOU SHARE WITH US THE STORY OF SELAH?

SHANNON: To give some context, our daughter Arrow was born right before Blake and I went to do our DTS in 2011. I got pregnant again when Arrow was nine months old and had a miscarriage fifteen weeks along in my pregnancy. We lost that baby, and I almost died. I had to get two blood transfusions— that was wild, but it wasn't traumatic for me. I understood that things like this happen sometimes. We decided to wait a little bit to try again. We prayed, sought the Lord and felt like He said, "Don't control getting pregnant. Just trust me in this area." I found out I was pregnant soon after that. We decided to officially move to Hawaii from North Carolina.

We got to Kona, Hawaii when I was about thirty-seven weeks pregnant. Suddenly, I stopped feeling the baby move. I thought something was wrong. We went to our local pregnancy center to get an ultrasound and they couldn't find the baby's heartbeat. We drove to the hospital immediately. We didn't cry or feel sad, we just believed the report of the Lord; we believed the baby would be born alive. We prayed earnestly the whole way to the hospital, "Lord, thank you for this baby. We speak life over our little girl." We were totally filled with faith. We let all of our friends know at the YWAM Kona campus and immediately the whole school was praying for our baby. People all over the world were praying. At the hospital, after the nurses and staff had done another ultrasound and had run tests on me, the doctor said, "Well, your baby is dead. We're going to induce you to get the baby out. You have to go through labor." I looked at him and told him, "Look, I just want you to know, we are believing for a miracle. We are believing that God will give us our baby alive." The doctor just laughed at us and walked out the door.

They induced me and I went through a very intense labor just as if I was going through birth normally. Mentally, it was pretty intense. When the doctors and nurses finally pulled the baby out, I didn't see her right away, but I remember looking down and seeing a knot in the umbilical cord. I started screaming and crying. I lost it. This is foggy for me, but they told us we had nine hours before they'd take her body to the morgue. So we held her and prayed over her body, that it would be raised from the dead. We did this for eight hours—some of our dear friends joined us. After all that time we finally let go.

The next day we went to a funeral home to pick out wood for her little casket. That moment was traumatic, crippling, damaging for my faith. My sister Melissa and her husband Jonathan flew out to Hawaii to be with us. We buried Selah in a public Hawaiian cemetery surrounded by seven close friends and family. I remember standing there; Andy, Jonathan and Taylor were digging her grave in the lava rock. That's when I first started feeling strong anger in my heart. Blake stood there that day and said, "The enemy will regret the day that he stole Selah from us."

WHERE DID YOU FEEL SADNESS AND PAIN THE MOST IN THE WEEKS TO FOLLOW?

SHANNON: The six weeks that followed were total hell. It was confusing. I was crying every day. I was angry. We were shocked. The questions started coming. *Why did this happen? Is God even real? He asks us to pray for the dead, but then He does whatever He wants anyway.* Our faith was challenged because we fought for something that God wanted us to fight for, but then the end result felt like there was no God at all. We still buried her. The pain of all of it was intense. Blake and I tried to pull ourselves together in the midst of arguing; we thought we might leave YWAM and move back home to North Carolina. We felt tricked by the Lord. We'd had wild faith for our family, and now we weren't sure we even heard Him. Sorting through those questions was more damaging to our faith than actually losing Selah.

BLAKE: I felt it in our marriage. I wanted to love my wife, but at the same time, we were both so heartbroken. The enemy was trying to take out our marriage, unity and belief. The weeks and months following was us rebuilding our trust and willingness to fight for our unity. We had to walk out our salvation again and establish unity. The enemy got really close to tearing us apart, but we were quick to get back on track.

SO, WAS THE GREATEST STRUGGLE FOR YOU BOTH THE ENSUING DOUBT?

SHANNON: Oh, yeah. The doubt came rushing in. We lost our assurance of faith. I remember driving around one night wrestling with God and just crying, crying, crying. We realized we were in a battle for our own faith and what we really believed.

WHAT WAS THE REVELATION THAT SPARKED HEALING AND CHANGE FOR YOUR MIND IN THE MIDST OF YOUR CRISIS?

SHANNON: One day I was in a YWAM meeting and a woman came in and sat down right beside us holding a newborn baby. I was flooded with anger. *God picks and chooses who gets to be alive and who doesn't.* I immediately left the meeting and went to my room. I laid in my bed and fell asleep, and God gave me a dream. I dreamed that there was a mountain, and people were walking, praying, reading their Bible, journaling and singing on the mountain. Everything in me shouted, "Get off the bed, get out of your anger and get on the mountain!" I looked up and saw Blake running furiously toward me. I sat up on the bed, pointed at him and called out, "The enemy is seeking to destroy us!" I woke up and immediately went to I Peter 5:8 and read, "Be alert and of sober mind. Your enemy the devil prowls around like a roaring lion looking for someone to devour" (NIV). The Holy Spirit spoke to me and said, "Shannon, I did not do this. I am the Giver of Life. There is no death in me. Your fight is not with me. Your fight is with the enemy. He hates you and your seed." I had the revelation that my "crisis of faith" wasn't about what God did or didn't do, but it was about recognizing that there is a real enemy who hates us, hates my marriage, my family and my children. What was really going on was that the enemy was trying to devour our faith and belief in God's goodness.

The truth is that God never puts us to shame. When I had that revelation, the anger and doubt immediately broke off of me. God was helping me understand His nature and get to the root of my disbelief. He didn't want me to just "get over it." He commanded me to rest. The enemy was seeking to devour Blake and I, just like he did to Job and so many others.

HOW DID THE LORD HELP YOU MOVE FORWARD?

BLAKE: It was a process for me to regain my belief and trust. I didn't have just one moment of revelation. The biggest thing for me was that I had some really amazing men around me—close friends—Andy Byrd being one of them. These guys would consistently ask me, "How are you doing? What sin is coming as a result of this situation? Is your disappointment turning into anger? Is your anger then turning to peace?" It's hard for me to find verbiage for my process, but the questions they asked me helped. Shannon's dream helped me in healing, too, but I didn't carry the dream of Selah the same way. When Shannon had her shift, I know it did help me some, but ultimately it was a process for me, not one moment. In order for fruit to unfold, the seed has to die, and I trusted the Lord through it all.

SHANNON: We learned how to trust the Lord and not question His goodness—we're not suspicious of His motives anymore. He revealed His true nature to us. If we don't know what God's really like, then we're always looking to our external circumstances and deciding if He's good or not. Every external reaction we have to the reality of Jesus is based on what we see or don't see Him do, like praying for people to be healed. God removed us of that—our opinion of Him that would constantly shift. Now, it doesn't matter. We know we gained the victory, because we lost another baby after Selah and it was nowhere near our past crisis. The enemy will no longer be able to sift us in that way again.

HOW DID YOU FIND COURAGE TO GET PREGNANT AGAIN?

SHANNON: We had a meeting with our friend Andy Byrd several weeks after Selah died. I was so angry and bitter, but we were still trying to engage in our roles at YWAM. Andy knew we were not doing well. He committed to having time with Blake to process Selah. He asked us when we would get pregnant again. Looking back now, I know it was a pivotal moment in my life—it was God that he asked us that. Andy charged us to not be led by fear in making the decision to get pregnant again. If we were afraid of getting pregnant, we needed to pray again. I use that model now for everything. Life is not about theology; it's about obedience to God. We must ask the Lord, and then genuinely do whatever He says.

So, not even two months after we buried Selah, we asked the Holy Spirit about getting pregnant; we both put fear behind us, and that was the week our son, Brave, was conceived. If we hadn't had that time with Andy and asked the Lord about getting pregnant, Brave wouldn't be here. God asked me, "Shannon, have you ever regretted following me? Have you ever wished I hadn't picked you?" And I couldn't think of one single time I regretted being His kid. Now, we look back, and it wasn't about a body living or dying. God gave us His perspective for our whole lives—it's about really knowing Him while we are here on this Earth. God settled it for us. When Brave was born, Melissa and I held him in our arms at the one-year mark of Selah's death. He was the son of redemption. He was the mark of God's power when we let go. It's changed our whole lives.

The Lord showed me that He has created me to swing for the fence every time. One of the greatest challenges I faced with Selah's situation was that I wished I had never believed she could be raised from the dead, because then I wouldn't be dealing with disappointment—not the disappointment of losing a child, but the disappointment and anger in God. But God showed me that I am called to believe big every time for any and every situation. Anytime someone comes to me and asks for prayer I am 100% going to swing for the fence; I'm an unshakeable force in truly believing that God can do anything. I'll be unpacking this for the rest of my life.

WHAT DID THE LORD TEACH YOU ABOUT STRENGTH IN THAT SEASON OF LOSS?

BLAKE: After Shannon's labor, when I was holding Selah in my arms in the hospital, I told the enemy that he would regret the day that he did this to our family. I've never been a big spiritual warfare guy; I've always focused on the Lord, but in that moment, I declared he would regret the day he robbed us.

As a father, I am not perfect. My kids know I'm not perfect. They also know I long to be like Jesus. I am quick to repent and fight for what Jesus would look like as a father to them. I've had major failings as a dad, but one thing Jesus said that always impacts me is, "The stone that the builders rejected has become the cornerstone...and the one who falls on this stone [Jesus] will be broken to pieces; and when it falls on anyone, it will crush him" (Matthew 21:42-44, ESV). Shannon and I always go back to our foundation; we're always falling on the cornerstone, Jesus, and we press into that being our strength. So, when I declared what I did in the hospital, even though the following weeks were pretty pathetic, our strength was walked out by our faithfulness. Our multiplication shows our kids that the enemy didn't have victory over us. When we are around young people we share these stories at the right time to increase people's faith, to show we have joy, which is our strength. The enemy tried to rob our faith, joy and strength, and was successful for a period of time; but the declaration stood stronger. For us, we share this testimony not as one of loss, but of the overcoming that came after. We chose to step into something uncomfortable.

DO YOU HAVE A WORD OF ENCOURAGEMENT TO SHARE FOR ANYONE WHO IS WALKING THROUGH THEIR OWN CRISIS OF FAITH?

SHANNON: The way God has unfolded His mercy and glory is more important than what actually happened to Selah. Deciding to stay in healthy community literally saved us. Being surrounded by people who knew the call of God on our lives saved us. Not isolating or choosing to be alone saved us. The Lord intervened, because we used wisdom in the midst of suffering. We've lost three children and buried two of those babies on the island of Kona. Even with our daughter Mighty, the miracle story of her being alive is crazy. If I could say anything it would be more than just us finding God in the midst of loss; what really happened is that God broke into our crisis and showed us what He is really like. I feel like I haven't lost anything at all. I know that sounds crazy, but the bottom line is I will never regret swinging for the fence. I'll never regret believing. I'll never regret the times I pray for things and people and circumstances that are important, regardless of what I see in the natural as a result. There is a greater faith that God has called us to carry that is beyond our external circumstances.

The greatest thing I want to communicate is to trust in the perfect love of the Father. We will die when we live with doubt. The only way to find out the truth is to go through the fire. We found out we weren't totally sure about who God was. We could've taken a very different path and not be in ministry, not be married, not have any more children. I wouldn't be the person known for faith that people come to for prayer for breakthrough. When I think about how thin that line was that we almost crossed, it really was a revival of our faith. Don't seek out the easy path anymore; take the path that transforms you into His likeness.

an anchor

for

the soul

Recipe for Imparting the Value of Hope to Your Children ——— Bethany Douglass

Artwork ——— Justina Stevens

"We have this as a sure and steadfast anchor of the soul, a hope that enters into the inner place behind the curtain, where Jesus has gone as a forerunner on our behalf..." (Hebrews 6:19-20, ESV).

Seven years ago our family had its financial legs swept out from under us by someone we trusted. It was dramatic, swift and painful. I still remember the morning light barely cresting the fence of our backyard, how blurry the future suddenly seemed, how heavy and palpable all of the unknowns felt. I did not feel afraid or angry; I felt small, watching castles turn to dust. A few months had passed, and I sat outdoors, reading these verses from Hebrews 6 aloud. Hope is an anchor for the soul—an anchor, secure and steadfast. I am embarrassed to admit that before that moment, the word *hope* seemed to me more appropriately cutout in bubble letters, something pinned to a Sunday school wall—naive and childlike, a wishful word tossed like pennies into a pond. Hope doesn't always feel like an anchor. Depending on the circumstance, hope can seem more like a raft, a fragile confidence, a flickering flame. Our circumstances, both the best and worst kind, appear so certain and firm in the moment, so final. They are so very easy to believe.

The writer of Hebrews calls faith "the substance of things hoped for and unseen" (Hebrews 11:1), and through this process in recent years, I am learning more deeply how faith and hope and love work together in each of us.

I am a planner. I can't help it. When circumstances happen as planned, I intuitively believe God is good because I feel good. I believe He is faithful because my plans happen accordingly. Without realizing it, God's goodness and character still exist within my own understanding. But He is so much more than what I understand. Hardships—those unsavory life experiences I prefer to avoid—are an invitation into the Father's plans, an invitation into His depth and breadth, into His love and faithfulness. There are believers in history who have understood hardship to be the signature of God's salvation in their life, so they have always made certain to belabor the point of hardship, to make sure they were not enjoying life on Earth too much. But hope is not the invitation into hardship; hope is what allows us to see hardship as an invitation. Hope builds an altar in the midst of the hardest of circumstances that says, "This is painful, but my God is more." Hope invites our hearts to believe; it activates our faith.

When our family's finances shifted suddenly, so did our circumstances. We sold everything, even our family home. Although I cried when we first decided to move, the decision was not a rash or hasty choice led by fear. My husband and I felt compelled, clothed in grace and strength and power. He bestows beauty for ashes, a garment of praise instead of despair (see Isaiah 61). Still, we trimmed every corner of our budget down, and seemed to use the word *no* more than ever, but we did so with hope, holding firm to the promises that the Lord would meet us. And He did—again and again. Although our four children were young at the time, it affected them, too. Moving them from a home and a space they loved was difficult, but it was also an opportunity to help them see how the Father would provide. When I imagined training our children to understand the Father heart of God, I didn't imagine

it this way. Perhaps I prefer the bubble letters and penny-tossing wishes. Clearly, the Lord had something different and better in mind. That, too, requires hope. We were transparent with our children through all of it though—not in a burdensome or overly detailed manner, but in a way that allowed them to see our faith, our submission to the King, our hearts open in forgiveness and blessing toward those who stole from us for their own gain. "Look at how the Lord has provided this!" we would say. "I would love to do that, too, let's ask the Lord for it." Sometimes it was a simple, "This is hard for me, too," or "What are you hoping for right now?" It goes without saying, but we are not perfect and this journey hasn't been either, but the Lord is carving deep trenches in each of us (children included) about His abundant heart toward us. He is more than we understand or imagine.

As modern first-world parents, it is humbling not to be all our children need. It seems culture tells us otherwise. Many of us want the best for our children, better than we want for ourselves, and I would suggest that desire is also a planting of the Lord, a seed of hope He means to cultivate. Sometimes what we want to give to our children in the form of things, the Lord means to grow in them through character and purpose. On the way home from a recent medical visit with our youngest, one of many to help repair her mouth after a trauma she incurred two months ago, she asked me about the future and what was to happen next. I looked at her again having to acknowledge I didn't know. I felt disheartened and frustrated. Then she turned to me with a bright and confident tone, so full of hope, and said, "It's okay, Mom. It's like Auggie's mom says in *Wonder* [her favorite book], 'The scars are only the map that show us where we've been.'"₅ Immediately, tears sprung to my eyes. Those words were for me. Those precious words, spoken with a toothless lisp, so full of hope and promise, so confident that her needs would be met, were for me. Sometimes our children are the ones the Father uses to remind us of hope and promise.

It seems nearly impossible to talk about hope without also acknowledging want. Desire. Longing. Dreams. The Father exists in those places of our hearts, too. We talk about these things often in our home, not in terms of our lack, but in terms of possibilities. Hope is not a wishful daydream or a passive glance to the skies outside our window. Hope is active, a defiant light in the dark, a weighty confidence in our Father-King: *I trust you; I believe your promise.* And so, I encourage anyone in need of hope to know God's promises toward you. Cling to them as a ship clings to an anchor in a storm.

Even our very desires—the want, the longing, all we perceive as want—begin with Him. They are an invitation for connection, an invitation to bring our deepest longings to Him, to talk with Him about them, to draw nearer to the Father and His purposes. He already knows. Yet the nearness to Him shapes us, transforms us. Shakespeare writes in *Hamlet*, "There is a divinity that shapes our ends, rough-hew them how we will."₆ We can trim and rough-hew our clay-like plans as we see best (and I regularly do), but it is our Father, with His deep affection for us and desire for us to know Him, who shapes our ends. He is a sure and steadfast anchor for our soul.

i
have
given
in

writing and photography
Melissa Helser

Recipe for: Opening Up
in Vulnerability
with your children

Oregon Coast, 2010

There is a love so deep in my soul that I didn't even know I was capable of...and every day it grows and surprises me. And my capacity for loving and teaching and forgiving and mothering keeps expanding, and I find myself really proud of myself. And then I find myself really proud of my kids. And then I erupt into thanksgiving. Because life is worth living. My kids are getting older. There is a joy and a sadness. I never knew I could love so much. I never knew I could give in so deeply to the human experience. I never knew that I could soften my heart over and over and let the rushing joy and tension of raising humans be my everyday. *I have given in.*

We travel a lot. Everywhere we go people comment about my kids. "They are so kind, so confident, so much fun." "You should have heard what Cadence said to me," or, "Haven is so perceptive of other people's needs." There is nothing more beautiful than people complimenting your children. It somehow reaches into the deep parts of your soul and unleashes an applause of epic proportion. The one thing you feel the most insecure about maybe isn't as bad as you think. Maybe you're winning at this parenting thing. Maybe all the things you pressed in to over and over actually stuck in the corners of their minds and maybe, just maybe, they were listening.

One of my favorite moments happened in May 2015, in Franklin, Tennessee. We were at a gathering leading worship. All weekend there was a lovely woman signing to a deaf man on the front row. My kids were taken by it the whole time. I would catch them watching her intently during the meetings; having never experienced anything like it, they were totally transfixed. When the last meeting was over and everyone was packing up, Cadence came up to me and casually told me that he had prayed for someone during the meeting. Surprised, I asked who. "Oh, the deaf man," he replied. He went on to do whatever he was on his way to do, and I stood there stunned. *Wow, I was not expecting that.* A few minutes

Cadence, age 8

Haven, age 5

later the interpreter came up to me: "Hey, do you have a minute? I want to tell you about something your son did." "Of course," I replied. What came next released an eternal smile in my mother's heart that I still think about to this day.

This is what she said: "Your son came up to me during worship and asked if I would interpret for him. He wanted to pray for my friend [the deaf man] and wanted to make sure that my friend understood what he was going to say. I agreed and followed him to where my friend was. He asked very graciously, 'Can I pray for you?' My friend agreed. Your son went on to pray for a solid ten minutes, prayers full of confidence and kindness. So tender and beautiful. I want you to know that I have been there for many years of many prayers, and I have never seen anyone pray with such hope and empathy. My friend was moved to tears and felt the prayer so deeply. You have an incredible son. Well done."

I stood there with tears streaming down my face. *My son...full of empathy.*

I have been sick my children's whole lives. They have been there when I could barely move, lying on the couch in so much pain. When I had major surgery on my feet, I was bed ridden for two months. Cadence sat on my bed every day, watching as the disease had taken its toll. They broke seven of my toes, fifty-four stitches. He sat with me every day. Every single morning, Haven asks me, "Mom, how did you sleep last night?" They have seen me cover my body because the psoriasis is so humiliating. They have protected me, defended me, fought for my heart and seen me in a way no other humans have had the capacity. They are my children, my offspring, my legacy. They are my reflection. I decided when Cadence was very little that I was not going to try to shield them from the pain; instead I would invite them in to it. Not to carry it or fix it but to learn one of the greatest gifts that humanity can learn—compassion.

When Cadence was little he would sit next to me at the park, on the steps of our house or on his bed, and he would rub one specific spot on my leg and pray over and over, "Jesus, heal my mommy." Recalling these memories floods my heart with so much emotion. It reminds me of the resilience that has been formed in my children. *They have learned that pain is real and sorrow is part of our experience, but the truer, more real thing is Hope.* This is not a trite, naive hope but a real, deep hope. They have seen me collapse from fatigue in moments where they knew I had nothing left and then rise to the occasion and press through. They have been there with me as I broke down crying, and they never try to fix it—they just wrap their arms around me and tell me they love me. I believe there is a beauty to the human experience, a fragility, a sorrow and a joy.

I believe that Jesus felt every range of human emotion. He went to the depths of loss, betrayal, disappointment, joy, celebration, delight. He felt it all, but He never broke connection to the Father. If He only did what He saw His Father doing, then He saw His Father weep and laugh and heal the sick and be a friend to the outcast. He watched His Father go to depths of the broken and needy, and there He found them transformed by the delight, approval and love of God.

The next morning after the conference, I woke up to the sound of giggling and the whispers of my two kids. We were all staying in the same room at a friend's house outside of Franklin. One of the joys of traveling with children is that most of the time we are all together in the same room. I sat up in bed to see them talking to each other, and I smiled and said good morning. They replied back with a joyful, "Good morning." Cadence's good morning smile quickly transformed into a peculiar look. "I had the most amazing dream," he murmured as he looked at me with a blank stare. The room filled with an expectation that is hard to put words to. By this time, Jonathan was awake, and we were attentive to whatever Cadence had to say. "I dreamt I was in a far away land, and I needed to get back home. I ran into Joel [our friend and drummer], and he said to me, 'Cadence, if you want to find your way back home, you need to go to

we cried together and it felt like magic in my soul.

the library and find the book that will take you home.' All of a sudden, I was in a large, old library looking for the book that would take me home. While I was walking through it, I heard a voice calling my name, 'Cadence, Cadence.' I went out of the library and walked down the hall, and there at the end of the hall was a large desk and God was sitting at it."

I want to interject here that the whole room was full of the presence of the Lord. We were all completely locked in to everything he was saying. Watching him process a dream in real time was incredible. We were all looking at him, and I asked, "Cadence did He speak to you?" "Yes, He did. He spoke to me." "What did He say?" I asked. Tears filled my twelve-year-old's eyes. The moment was full of the glory of God. We waited and didn't push. "He said, 'Cadence I am so proud of you for praying for that deaf man. You are so brave; I am so proud of you.'"

It is one thing to tell our children we are proud of them, but it is something entirely different for the Father to reach into our parenting and tell them He is proud of them. We all live for the Father's approval, His delight. We all live for the "*well done.*" I have very few words for the power of that moment. You see, I don't know if that precious man was healed that night, but that wasn't really the goal. Is it not as much of a healing to the soul to receive the kindness, compassion and empathy of another human, let alone a child? His tears flowed because he felt the true tenderness of Father God in a young man. Then God the Father visited my son in a dream to tell him, "I am proud of you." Not for getting the job done, but for reflecting His true nature.

My kids are soft and strong. When they cry we join in the chorus, and when we cry they draw in close. Just the other night I sat down at the piano and Cadence, my now sixteen-year-old, sat next to me. We played together like we did when he was young. Tears streamed down my face the moment he sat down, and after forty-five minutes of melodies swirling around us, I stopped and whispered, "You're getting older, and it makes me sad." He wrapped his huge arms around me and whispered back, "I know, Mom. I am sad, too." We cried together, and it felt like magic in my soul.

I will never apologize for my tears. They come not because I am hopeless, but because I am alive. I am constantly asking the Lord for strength to know where to let my children in and where to protect...lately I let them in more. I have found that is what is really protecting them: my vulnerability and willingness to be weak in front of them and in front of Father God. I am not a perfect parent, but that was never the goal.

May you, the reader, feel the overwhelming permission to ask the Holy Spirit where to let your children in. Where to give them a window into your pain and let them experience the depths of need. I truly believe we have the grace to teach our kids what it means to live a healthy, brilliant life, but life is full of suffering. This is not a heavy thing, but a beautiful, deep experience. One that pulls us into the stunning grace and life of Jesus. I pray you feel liberated to be real and sensitive with your kids. To teach them empathy by example and lead them to the feet of Jesus in every moment of life.

the PRIORITY IS

CONNECTION

An Interview on Communication and Collaboration
with Jason & Lauren Vallotton

By Allie Sampson & Erin Gravitt
Photography from Personal Collection,
Sydnee Mela & Morgan Campbell

Jason and Lauren Vallotton have been married over six years and both work on the Leadership Team at Bethel Church in Redding, California, an incredible community of believers passionate about God's manifest presence. In his role, Jason oversees all the departments and ministries that are aimed at emotional health and pastoral care. Lauren is Director of Operations, helping the church strategize and develop projects while bringing leadership direction to their movement. They are both pastors spending a large portion of their days counseling and training staff.

We sit down with this extraordinary married couple inside the new Art Barn at the Farm during a beautiful fall day to hear their story. The sunlight streams through the windows, casting light on Lauren's face as she speaks through laughter and tears about her journey through becoming a new wife and mother all at once. Jason's kind, steady glances at her affirm again and again the rock he has been for her amidst such rapid life transition. This beautiful blended family is changing a generation with their faithful love and consistency. Join us on this dive into the depths of courage and risk. Like the Vallottons, may you find yourself prioritizing revolutionary ways to connect to those you love most through the simple, humble act of trust.

CAN YOU TELL US A BIT ABOUT YOUR LOVE STORY?

LAUREN: Oh, our love story is so good. We crossed paths a lot at Bethel because of our mutual friend, and I got a phone call from Jason one evening to go on a walk. That night, Jason, on our first ever one-on-one hang out says, "Well, I'd like to tell you where my heart's at. I don't actually do this. I don't actually take girls out and hang out with them one-on-one. And so I just want to be clear: I'm interested in pursuing you. Would it be okay with you if I pursued your heart?" Truthfully, I felt like I had been in a few dating relationships that I had accidentally fallen into; I didn't feel like I had ever dated well. I really wanted a healthy, beautiful relationship built on trust. So, when he came out of the gate being so clear in his communication, speaking so clearly to me about his intentions, why would I say no? But in the back of my head, I didn't know how long our dating relationship could actually go, because he's been divorced and has three kids. That's just not anybody's dream—to marry a guy that's been divorced and has kids. I ended up saying yes, because I was interested in him. If I had really thought about all the implications in that moment, I don't know if I would have said yes. Anyway, we hung out every day from that point forward!

JASON: Our relationship was different because I had kids. In order to actually date a woman, I first needed to make sure my kids were alright with it. They were young at the time; my oldest son, Elijah, was ten, my daughter Riley was eight, and Evan was five years old. I had already talked to them ahead of time, asking, "Hey, this is what I'm thinking about doing. Are you okay with it?" We let the kids determine the bench-markers in our relationship so they weren't confused. I also wanted to leave Lauren a lot of

room to breathe while we were dating. I remember telling her one night, "If you can't see your dreams growing by saying yes to marrying me, then don't say yes to me. I want to marry you, but I don't want you to feel like you are missing an opportunity to partner with somebody else who brings you joy."

LAUREN: On paper, I think it looked like my life was getting reduced to being a step-mom of three children; it might have looked like I was giving up the world. But I genuinely got to a place in my heart where I felt like saying no to marrying Jason was an option, but saying yes to being his wife felt like this huge, expansive opportunity.

LAUREN, YOUR STORY IS REALLY UNIQUE. WHAT DID IT LOOK LIKE TO SAY YES TO BECOMING A MOM OF THREE? WHAT HAS THAT PROCESS BEEN LIKE FOR YOU?

LAUREN: Oh, tears! (*Laughing and tearing up simultaneously.*) It has been so beautiful and so hard. Mothering is how I'm wired. It was second nature for me to come into something that was a mess, clean it up, bring some structure and mother the kids— that felt like breathing to me. What I did not anticipate was, in the process of learning how to be a mom, encountering my own fears that I didn't know I had. You can't know your real fears until you're under an amount of pressure or stress. I always say that my hardest moments in parenthood were not ever because of the kids—they were the easy part. They've gotten older now, and having teenagers has been interesting; but when we first got married, they were pretty young. Learning how to make space for all these new people who had needs was difficult. I didn't realize for the first couple of years that I was carrying so much pressure and responsibility to be the rescuer—to save everyone all the time. For the first couple of years, I think I just powered through on adrenaline; then the next two years was recovering from all that! It wasn't until four years into being a wife and mom that I started to finally get a grip on my fears needing to die. I knew I needed to learn how to operate in peace apart from anxiety. It has been such a journey. If you're looking from the outside, you would think that we were kicking butt—and we were on a lot of levels, but there was so much grace to do it. It was still the hardest thing I've ever done.

LAUREN, WHAT WAS IT LIKE TO ENTER INTO THE VALUE SYSTEMS THAT JASON HAD IN PLACE FOR PARENTING ALREADY? AND JASON, HOW DID YOU WELCOME LAUREN INTO BOUNDARIES YOU ALREADY HAD FOR YOUR KIDS?

LAUREN: Being a blended family has been easy because of Jason doing the thing you just said. He paved such a way for me to come in and learn for the first little while. He did all the heavy lifting when it came to discipline or setting priorities for the kids. I got to watch, learn and adopt. Learn how their normal worked, because we were pretty aware that it wasn't going to work for me to come in and switch everything up. I had to learn that in their home the priority was connection above everything else. What I learned right away from Jason is that even in discipline, connection is the goal. I really became a student of parenting by watching Jason. He is an incredible dad.

JASON: When you're blending a family, you're not necessarily starting over. You already have some momentum. At the same time, you are adding new. For starters, the kids loved Lauren as their mom. They called her Lauren-mom, and then Mom at home, which gave her permission to slowly give input, correction and direction in their lives. We established that if one parent said one thing, the other parent backed it up whether we agreed with it or not, and then we'd talk about it later. Our kids weren't put before her in our marriage; that's a big mistake that a lot of blended families make. The kids end up getting in between step-mom or step-dad, and then we end up trying to protect a certain child from the other parent. When we were dating we agreed that the kids came first, but the day that we got married, Lauren became first. That was a message that was communicated to the kids in a very loving, kind way. So, they were able to come under our authority, and they've never one time said to Lauren, "You're not my mom."

THERE'S NO FORMULA FOR RAISING PERFECT KIDS. CAN YOU SHARE ANY SPECIFIC KEYS THAT THE HOLY SPIRIT HAS GIVEN YOU TO OVERCOME MOMENTS OF DIFFICULTY IN PARENTING?

JASON: For me, the key has been community. Lauren and I have a counselor that we go to regularly, and the kids go to the same counselor. Our kids will set up their own appointments if they feel like they need to talk. That's really normal for our family. My oldest son will call his grandpa and work stuff out with him. And then my dad will give me helpful feedback, too. In parenting, there's a lot of confusion, pain and frustration sometimes. The main thing for us is keeping our connection, which is the priority. And then, if we can't figure out what to do we talk through it with other people.

LAUREN: I would say that a key is raising kids who learn how to value and articulate what's going on inside of their own hearts. You don't get connection unless you know how to communicate. Jason really taught the kids how to validate and honor what's going on inside of their hearts, which made room for communication. As parents, we help minimize the pain by giving our kids the tools that they need to establish connection. A lot of relationship breakdown happens, especially with teenagers, because people were never taught how to communicate and keep connection through disagreement and conflict. You end up with parents and teenagers who don't know how to interact with each other. Give children communication tools when they are young, so that when they do get older and have their own opinions and ideas, you can talk through it. You have to give their hearts language.

Kids have a billion "why" questions. It's easy to say, "Because I said so," but we don't actually have a real reason. One time Elijah asked why he had to go to bed so early: "That's so unfair! My friends get to stay up as late as they want." Jason grabbed the white board and marker and sat down with Elijah; he drew out for him a detailed explanation of why he has to go to bed at ten o'clock. This was all about protecting connection. Jason explained, "You have to go to bed by ten tonight, because in the morning we need to be able to have good connection. I need you to not be tired and grumpy. My whole goal is that you'd grow up and be a man and move out of this house; that you'd be able to fulfill your dreams in connection with family. If I let you do whatever you want here, then later in life, you're going to be this individualistic person unable to do connection with community..." He went on and on mapping this whole big thing together, but it was beautiful! It actually helped Elijah to understand that there's a legitimate reason that we need him to go to bed at a reasonable time. That's a funny, long example! It's not like every conversation is that long and involved, but we do try really hard to help the kids understand the heart issue behind the values we have, and not just the surface.

WHAT HAVE YOUR KIDS SURPRISINGLY TAUGHT YOU IN SIMPLE, EVERYDAY MOMENTS?

JASON: Man, a lot. I look at my kids and see how patient God is with us. Being a parent requires so much patience. I think parenting has taught me to trust the Lord when I don't want to; to give up things that I don't want to give up. There's beauty and sacrifice.

LAUREN: They have taught me how to love people who are very different than me. All of my boxes have been shattered by these little people. They didn't know they were doing it, but they did—they broke all my boxes. It's the kindness of God to do that quickly for me. It could have taken years for me to walk into a space that was really open and free. I'm grateful in hindsight that God did that in a short, condensed period of time rather than dragging it out, because I know I'm going to live so much more free than I would have been if I'd have stayed in my little boxes.

IF YOU ALL COULD SHARE ONE WORD OF ENCOURAGEMENT TO PARENTS WHAT WOULD YOU SAY?

LAUREN: I would say that Jesus cares way more about their children's wellbeing, success and hearts than we as parents ever could. So give yourself a break, and do not feel like all the pressure of raising your kids is on you to figure out. Your children are the Lord's; He is so faithful to keep them. God has got them, and we are not their saviors. We get to help shape and lead them, but ultimately, they are the Lord's. The pressure is off.

JASON: Kids are so much more resilient than we think that they are. Parents do make a lot of mistakes, they totally do. There's a lot of shame and regret for the mistakes that we make, but I know that through love, care and community, kids have such a great capacity to weather storms and bounce back. They are able to persevere more than we think. There is always a beautiful path to restoration, love and protection for them.

HONOR

CULTIVATING FRIENDSHIP
WITH YOUR PARENTS

"Honor your father and your mother, so
that you may live long in the land the Lord
your God is giving you." Exodus: 20:12

3 GeneratiONS.

Recipe for Generational Freedom ——— Jonathan David Helser

Photograph ——— Personal Collection

I have always been fascinated that one of the names of God we see throughout the Scripture is: the God of Abraham, Isaac and Jacob. It's incredible that God wanted to be eternally known as the God of three generations. Not one generation, but three. The God of a grandfather, a father and a son. Since my firstborn son, Cadence, came into our world, I have had the extraordinary privilege of experiencing three generations living in community together. My father and I are next-door neighbors and have done ministry and life together since Cadence was born. The time has moved so fast; Cadence is sixteen years old and is already six feet three inches. Right now we are the exact same height, but I am just waiting for the day I look into his eyes and realize he has outgrown me. I know that day is coming soon, not just in the natural, but also in the Spirit. That's how God planned for it to be. Sons standing taller than their fathers and going beyond what their fathers ever dreamed.

Since Cadence was a little boy, he has had such a special friendship with my dad. One of his favorite things to do with my dad is work outside. From mowing grass on the tractor, to planting seeds in the garden, my dad and Cadence have spent many hours enjoying the beauty of working the land together. I am so thankful my son has gotten to experience this with my dad. He is one of the most extraordinary men I have ever met. He has the remarkable gift of being a creative visionary with the ability to dream huge dreams, while also having the heart of a servant king, always willing to pour out his life and work with all his might to see those dreams become a reality. Our ministry, A Place for the Heart, would not be here if it wasn't for my dad's whole-hearted devotion. Cadence has learned so much by spending time with his "Papa" when they work together. I know my dad is passing his legacy

Cadence, Ken + Jonathan, 2002

to the next generation, through hard work and sweat, skills and stories, wisdom and humor that come from walking and working side by side.

When Cadence was ten years old, he was helping my dad finish a big project at his house. Every afternoon Cadence would join his Papa after school and they would work till dinner each night. Each evening, Cadence would come home tired but full of stories to share around the dinner table of all he learned while working with his Papa. One of those days, Cadence came home and said, "Dad, you and Papa are so much alike, especially when you get stressed. You guys both huff the exact same way when you are overwhelmed." I instantly laughed at this reality and also tried to not get too offended as my son helped me see the truth about myself. Children are an amazing mirror to reflect back to parents who they are.

Later that weekend, we were rushing out the door as a family to make an important engagement. It was one of those days when everything seemed to go wrong: the kids couldn't find their shoes, the car keys were missing and the dog had peed on the floor. When we finally all got in the car and were headed down the road, Cadence spoke up from the back seat, "Hey Dad, the whole time we were trying to leave the house, you have been doing that huffing thing again, just like Papa." In the moment, I kind of felt like I was getting pulled over by the cops. I will admit I was a bit irritated, but I was also thankful and I decided to give in to the truth and let it set me free. I also was ready to help Cadence see how much he is just like me and his granddad. I caught his glance in the rearview mirror and said, "You are right Cadence. I was way too stressed the last twenty minutes. I'm sorry." And then I asked, "Cadence did you know that you also huff when you're stressed, like I do?" He was a bit taken aback by this and instantly responded, "No I don't." I laughed and said, "Well let's just wait and see about that." It was hardly five minutes later when one of his legos fell under a crack in the seat and he couldn't find it. A familiar sound rose from the backseat as Cadence's exasperated huffing rang out. "What's happening back there Cadence?" I asked. "I can hear you huffing and puffing loud and clear." He had been caught, just like I had been earlier, and we all started laughing. Then I asked Cadence a question, "Who huffs more: your Papa or me?" He instantly responded, "Definitely Papa. He huffs way more than you do, Dad." I smiled and said, "That's right, and what's so amazing is you are going to huff less than I do."

Peter Scazzero says, "Jesus may be in your heart, but grandpa is in your bones."[7] This is a truth that might make you cry one minute and then laugh the next. I have watched this unfold over and over again in our day-to-day lives among three generations. I have learned to lay down my judgments and criticism of the next generation and humble my heart to learn from them. I have made it a practice to stay thankful for all that the generation ahead of me has given. This practice has developed a deep compassion and understanding in my heart for who my parents are and for who I am as a parent. I can't put into words how grateful I am for my parents. They laid down so much of their lives so that their ceiling could be my floor. They made a way for me to go further than they could, and now, I get to take what I learned from them to build a floor for my kids. Every time I look at the generations that went before me and make intentional choices to go beyond them, to fight for a better way, the more I am setting my kids up for success. The reality is, Cadence will go further than I've gone. My sincere hope is that, when he is my age, he will have freedom, understanding and healthy belief systems that I didn't even know were possible. Watching him turn my ceiling into his floor is the greatest reward of my life. It is what makes the work of transformation worth it—that every generation far surpasses the last.

THE COLLECTOR

Recipe for Treasuring ———— Phyllis Unkefer

Photograph ———— Personal Collection

My father kept all the elementary school clay creations that my brother, sister and I made: the wobbly pinch pots, the rainbow-striped tigers, a fat bald eagle in a lopsided nest. He kept them on a shelf in the upstairs of our barn, between all his books, toolboxes and harmonicas. I still like to look at them when I visit home. Because he's kept them, they've quietly transformed from our crooked and unshapely attempts at art into a shelf full of his affection.

In some ways, my dad was reserved. Direct expressions of endearment—like a candid "I love you"—weren't common. That is, not until the last year of his life, when cancer brushed up against his mortality and loosened his voice. All sorts of new and shocking declarations came across the bridge of his tongue. "I love you" turned into a greeting. His prayers were confided out loud with tenderness. Once when there was bad news at a doctor's appointment, he announced, "I'm standing on the Rock, and the Rock is *Christ.*" This astonished my twenty-two-year-old heart, which had wondered about his beliefs for years. When I was in high school, my family fought frequently, as do many families in seasons of pain—everyone trying to be heard, but rarely hearing. At that time, it was hard to hear my father's heart beyond the turmoil, but hindsight with the Holy Spirit brings clarity. I look back to realize that while he was reserved, he stated his fondness in other ways.

When I visit my childhood home, I can see all the things my father built. The white shelves in my bedroom. The fire pit in the woods. The entire back deck, where in the summer, Zydeco swelled from a tape player while we laughed over card games, slinging accusations at the cheater who was schooling us all at Spoons. He built a two-story barn for a garage with enough space to fit a trampoline in the back. Here we did flips and seat wars, and he, having been a gymnastics coach, waved in the neighborhood kids who peeked through the door and begged to be taught the Swivel Hips again. When I touch the trampoline's springs, it feels like fondness to me. I don't know what it is about *things,* physical objects, that can retain so much significance. As if somehow, emotion can get caught inside them and stay drenched there like an overwatered flowerpot. These things, the works of his hands, speak to me. I walk around the house and listen. There is still a clearing in our backyard where the tree fort he built used to stand. It had swings, and there was no escaping the rope burn on my clutched hands when

his underdog pushes felt like rocket ships launching, felt like my feet were glancing off the sky, felt like joy tap-dancing in my chest.

My dad helped construct our new dining room, the room where we rehearsed my mission trip fundraising concerts so I could chase Jesus around Asia (concerts that were his idea, and at which he lit up everybody's eyes with a blues harmonica solo to *God Put a Rainbow in the Sky.*) And there's our house itself, which he, unbeknownst to me, put a second mortgage on just so I could attend an arts boarding school when I was seventeen. I walk around this house and listen, because it speaks his heart to me.

There's more than what I can now touch and see. Memories of when he came to all of my games, nodding assurance from the basketball bleachers or doing cartwheels down the soccer field sidelines, potbellied but agile nonetheless. I've collected the bits of advice he offered me in my preteen years: *never cut toward yourself with a knife; drive twenty-five miles per hour in a neighborhood to care for the kids; always keep a friend's secret.* His words were full of the conviction that I was worthy enough to live them.

There is a patchwork of my father's affection that I sew together in my memories. I stand in front of this shelf of warped pottery, and I feel the same way I felt at age fifteen when he reminisced about the day I lost my first tooth. "You remember that?" I asked, with wide eyes from the passenger seat. "Yes," he said, "I remember your *whole life.*"

When I stand in front of this shelf, I am silent. Warmth starts in my sternum and slowly spreads through me, till it gathers in pools just below my ribs, till it seeps over my shoulders and swims behind my eyes. Till *I'm* the watered flower. When I stand here in front of this shelf, I feel *treasured.* To treasure is "to keep carefully; to value highly." God Himself treasures, collecting even our tears. Treasuring, I've learned, is a generous act; treasuring begets treasuring. A few weeks after my father passed away, I walked through our house treasuring the work of his hands. And I found, at this shelf of old clay figurines, that he also treasured mine.

Prompt: The Father is a collector. Psalm 56:8 (NLT) says, "You have collected all my tears in your bottle. You have recorded each one in your book." Ask Him, "Father, how have you treasured me? What have you collected from my life?" Journal His response. Then imagine a new way you can begin to treasure someone you love.

the golden threads

Recipe for Growing Gratitude for Your Parents ——— *Melissa Helser*

Photography ——— *Personal Collection*

It's the end of March, sunny, sixty-five degrees. Joy rushes through my soul as I open every window in my house. A strange, familiar feeling rushes over me. Memories of my mother flood my mind...she would always open every window and let the house fill with air of the new season. Always making space for lovely moments in our home. So many things I learned from her. They slip into my mind with effortless beauty and take me by surprise. I owe so much of my rhythms and loves to my mother. When I was young I had no idea how to appreciate them, but now I love and practice so many of them regularly.

My clearest memory of my mom was looking out my bedroom window of our two-story house on a Sunday afternoon. She would be there in a canvas-woven lawn chair, stretched out sunbathing, resting, napping. My father respected her Sabbath so much. She didn't cook or clean or tend to much. She is a mother of five and spent her weeks loving, caring, cooking, cleaning, driving

us from one place to the next. So Sundays...they were sacred. I remember opening my window in the spring and feeling the breeze blow through my bedroom as I burned the image of my mother resting in the front yard on my mind. I replay that image a lot. She knew how to give it all and then let it all go. She practiced rhythms of beauty and consistency. Always teaching us to love hard, play hard and rest hard. I am realizing in my late thirties that my mom is most definitely one of my heroes. A true lover of life and God and all that is beauty. She taught me to love long walks, sunsets, good wholesome food, the wind, fresh flowers, laughter, parties, hosting, teaching, sitting on the beach for hours, lakes, boats, my children...I could go on and on and on. As I get older it seems that I have more and more capacity to let all the beauty in, and with it comes thanksgiving and compassion.

It is so important in the midst of reflecting back on our childhoods that we remember the good and not just the hard. As adults it's so easy to get caught up in everything our parents didn't give us and miss the beauty that was there. I learned in my twenties to find the Golden Threads. They are the things that keep moving through the years and give beauty and color and depth to our lives. Without them, we wouldn't have roots that reach back, back, back…into the heritage of who we are. The Golden Threads are the skeleton of who we are. They make up so much of our structure. Of course we don't want to take everything our parents gave us into the way we live. That wouldn't actually honor their process of becoming more and more whole. We should absolutely move and grow beyond them. That is maturing.

I can say that lately, I have practiced spending more time thanking God for the simple things that shaped me and molded my heart. Praying for empathy and compassion. Looking at my parents and realizing that they gave me what they had…it wasn't everything I needed, no parent can do that. Only the Father, Son and Holy Spirit give me everything I need. Finding the Golden Threads keeps me focused on the beauty of what I have been given and gives me the courage to let go of all that does not need to remain.

We live life from season to season, growing deeper and higher. It is so valuable to ask the Holy Spirit to show us the beauty that should remain and reveal the things we want to let go of. Honoring our parents by becoming the best version of our true self. Living in denial isn't going to change us and neither is living in bitterness. We must find the balance of being honest with our own hearts about the deficiency that we all had and truly let the Lord in to parent those places. As I grow and become older, I practice writing down two lists. The first is of the beautiful aspects of my life. It changes with every season, not what actually happened, but the way I see it and remember it. As I mature, I give memories space to be different. I write down all the things about my mom and dad that I love—the threads I want to preserve and let work their way through my life, into my children and their children. I want to look at my kids as adults one day and know that parts of them are just like my mother and her mother. It is how I honor what has been while continuing forward.

The second list is the things I want to let go of. Compiling this list takes the courage my mother imparted to me when I was young. I cannot complete this without the friendship and support of the Holy Spirit, letting Him flood my heart with His thoughts about my parents. When I invite Him, I can write in compassion instead of judgment. It is still so real and I feel the pain of moments, cycles, patterns but I don't feel the intense residue of criticism. I can see that my mother gave me what she had been given and truly became a more beautiful version of herself. She was more whole than my grandmother and I will be more whole than her and Haven, my daughter,

will be more whole than me. And that is how we grow and honor the generations of struggle, pain, glory and triumph. I keep letting go…and I keep holding on. I keep choosing love and keep embracing honesty. I will not live a life of denial but I also will not live a life of bitter judgment casting my criticism on those that tried to love me the most. My parents were not perfect…but that was never the point.

I sit in the light and breeze of an open window and thank God for a mother who taught me to appreciate the simple things in life. To savor the every day and live my life on purpose…mostly for my family. I forgive and let go of all the things I know I needed and didn't get, and commit in joy to parenting out of a place of growth and not out of a place of "I am going to be everything my kids need." That mentality is impossible. The more I get honest with myself and my story, the more I forgive my parents, the more I can forgive myself. My kids will one day make the list. And they will grow beyond me. They will grow beyond my perfectionism, my huffing, my impatient behavior. Mostly because they are hearing me say I am sorry, and watching me give in to growth. They know I am committed to becoming my true self, and that takes time. My honor is their growth. My legacy is their wholeness.

Prompt: Sit down with the Holy Spirit. Ask Him to fill your heart with compassion, empathy and joy. Ask Him to show you the Golden Threads, the beauty that you want to take with you into your rhythms of life. They can be anything. Super simple or really profound. For example, I want to take my mother's passion and love for the broken as much as I want to keep her love for flowers and open windows. I practice not overthinking it but letting the beauty fill my mind. Then I ask Him for help again. "Holy Spirit, show me the things I am meant to grow beyond in honor, not judgment." I write down patterns, cycles, little things that stick out to me to let go of. For example, I don't want to carry my mother's worry or the way she handled being overwhelmed. In compassion, I have so much space to be honest and pray for my mom and actually see that she is a different person in her sixties than she was when I was a teenager. I can love her in the now and not be chained to judgments I have about my childhood, but I also can be honest and grow beyond, so that I can engage my teenagers with a different capacity.

As you're making the list, don't stress if it's only a few things. Let it be whatever it is. When I first did this it felt charged and intense, like I was going in and tearing out. Similar to the moments when we "Spring Clean" in stress. I am learning before I sit down and write to ask the Holy Spirit to give me eyes to see. In every season the Holy Spirit will lead you to what He desires to reveal. Practice trusting Him. Practice forgiving. Practice letting go, and most of all practice holding on.

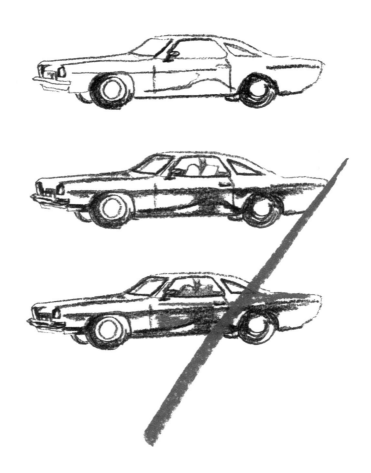

Seven Seconds

Recipe for Learning the Hearts of our Parents ——— Jason Upton

Artwork ——— Justina Stevens

When I was a little boy, I rode shotgun with my dad in his 1970s Oldsmobile Cutlass Supreme since there weren't any laws prohibiting that in the 70s. I would hold his hand in the front seat of his car, and we would sing songs together and tell stories. On longer drives my dad would ask me, "What do you want to be when you grow up?" I told him all sorts of answers: a fireman, a policeman, a garbageman, a doctor, the President of the United States of America. My dad would always ask me for a detailed explanation, "Why a garbageman?" I told him I wanted to be the kind of garbageman who was able to ride on the back of the dump truck holding on with one hand, as this was a common sight in the suburbs of Minneapolis at the time. My dad would have responded, "You mean, you wouldn't want to drive the truck? You'd rather be the guy holding on, eh?" On and on the dialogue would continue until we reached our destination. When we arrived at our destination, my dad rarely opened his door until he was sure our conversation was over, and no matter how wild my dreams were, he would always smile at me and say, "It's possible!"

A few years ago my parents came to our home for a visit. My dad and I went to go run some errands. "I'll ride shotgun," my dad said. My dad, in his late 60s, had just recently retired, so as I drove him around, I asked him what he was thinking about doing in his retirement. He replied, "I've decided to learn to be a guitarist." Knowing how difficult this would be for him to learn for the first time at sixty-seven years old, I was quiet. He continued, "Jason, one day I want to be a really, really great guitar player. I've been practicing every single day, and I think I've got a shot at it. Who knows, maybe one day I'll play with you." I remained silent; all I could think about was how difficult this would be for him—it actually seemed impossible! We both said nothing for a few seconds; then my dad looked at me with a big smile on his face and broke the awkward silence, "But, no pressure, Jason."

The next day I was reminiscing about that moment. My mind began recalling all the memories I had of riding with him, sharing my dreams. I remembered how he would always encourage me by saying, "It's possible." My eyes filled with tears as I heard the voice of the Holy Spirit say, "Your father shared his dream with you." I don't think anyone willingly misses an opportunity to respond properly when his or her dad opens up his heart. As much as I would have wanted to respond properly and kindly to my dad in that moment, I realized I wasn't well-practiced at responding to my dad sharing his dreams with me. The secret to my dad's "it's possible" response was that it wasn't a spontaneous reaction; rather, it was disciplined, prepared and intentional. My dad thought long and hard about how he was going to respond to his dreamer of a boy. I imagine there may have been a few awkward moments of silence in the beginning of our car ride conversations whereupon he might have thought, "I need to respond better to my son. I can't just remain silent when he shares his dreams with me. How will I respond the next time this happens? What is the best kind of response that I can offer my son?" He arrived at this: "It's possible."

I had about seven seconds to respond to my dad that day in the car before he so graciously broke the awkward silence. That's about as much time as any of us will ever have to respond appropriately in moments like these with those we love. One of the coolest parts of this story is that, even when I didn't know what to say, my dad knew what to say. He was practiced. His attitude toward me said, "It's okay, son. You can take your time in responding. You don't have to know what to say right now."

Spontaneity isn't a form. Spontaneity is the reality of any living relationship. When asked how he continued to capture the perfect photograph, renowned landscape photographer Ansel Adams quoted Louis Pastuer: "Chance favors the prepared mind."[8] Adams would study a shot for hours, waiting to see what the unpredictable light, shadows, and weather patterns would do; he would wait for the spontaneous, chance moment to click the shutter.

Like Adams, I want to capture these moments when they arise. Sadly, often the moment arrives, and I'm so surprised by it that I forget to click the shutter! Knowing how to respond properly in our relationships requires a commitment to studying the people we love the way Adams studied the landscapes. There really isn't another way to learn other than the way my dad learned, and then we adjust our responses accordingly. There is no surrogate for intimacy. Our relationships are living, unique and spontaneous. The key is studying the landscape of these relationships long enough so that we're ready to respond properly to the wonderful moments as they happen. In other words, click the shutter!

Prompt: One of the most spontaneous moments in the Bible is the story of the Lost Son (see Luke 15). Read the text aloud. Notice how the boy prepares his remarks for his father. Then notice the unpredictable, spontaneous and merciful way the father responds to his son's return. The father's response broke all the rules of the day, yet it was the proper response in the moment. Pray this prayer: "Father, thank you that you are fully prepared to respond to us with belief and kindness every moment of our lives. I may be shocked and caught off guard by your mercy, but you always know what you're going to do and say, for you are the Living God." Now, ask the Lord for some ways you can practice having a "prepared mind" for spontaneous moments of interaction with your parents, spouse, children, neighbors and friends. Journal His voice.

Great Aunt Ida, Lucille Harvey, Great Aunt Bertha, mid 1970's

unlikely fruit

Recipe for Embracing Your Legacy ———— Phyllis Unkefer

Photograph ———— Personal Collection

My Great Aunt Ida's backyard was a garden. This would not be an extraordinary detail, except that she lived just a block from the busy, highly populated city of Detroit, Michigan. She had an urban garden decades before the current trend. If you walked around the corner, you'd see it through the chainlink fence: daffodils, grapevines, tulips and sweet potatoes, erupting like laughter. My Great Aunt Ida lived 104 years and spent seventy of those close to the soil, fingers combing the ground, dragging up weeds, persuading a water hose and cupping the fragile chins of flowers. She was a farm girl from Georgia with a raspy, generous laugh. In the African-American migration to the north in the 1930s, she moved to a rural township outside of Detroit. As decades passed and the city stretched out its cement arms, its sprawling auto factories, its car exhaust, she kept on planting life.

On my dresser, there's a photograph of her standing in front of her garden in a dark blue dress. I've kept it there ever since the night I saw her in a dream. I dreamt she owned a town house in New York City with a tiny, boxed-in backyard. The yard was wedged between skyscrapers that towered on all sides, but she'd still somehow planted a garden. She grew banana trees, mangos, pineapples and all sorts of unlikely fruits. Their flourishing in the buildings' shadows seemed like an impossibility. When I woke up that morning, I heard the Father whisper to me, "This is your legacy."

Unlikely fruit. Many women in my Great Aunt Ida's family have been just this, including her sister, my Grandmother Ora. She died before I was born, but I've heard stories and side-notes about her—that she loved grapefruit. That she wrote letters back and forth to my grandfather before they ever met. That though she was usually reserved, her *soul got happy* one Sunday, and she danced wild, flying hands and feet, inside a little storefront church. She made the brave and uncertain exodus from Georgia to Detroit in the early 1940s, when the things committed against her race were too terrorizing to stay. To be unlikely fruit, you must choose to grow where it doesn't seem that you can.

My grandmother was a poor, black country girl, and though it was uncommon at the time, she graduated from college. She married, had four children and lived through her first stroke by the time she was fifty-five. Her second stroke left her arm and leg paralyzed, as if one whole side of her body were a house where all the lights had gone out. By then, her husband had taken to drinking, no doubt encouraged by the unforgiving confines of a job on a factory assembly line. His temper swelled and stormed with alcohol, so they often fought. And for years, there was a heavy river of depression that flowed through my grandmother's mind, a fitful sadness that settled on her soul for stretches of time. It's in the midst of this pain that Ora planted unlikely fruit.

Legacy takes root in a thousand small choices. My grandmother loved God deeply. She gave her trust to Him through a thousand yeses. Yes, every morning she woke up and exercised her paralyzed leg. Yes, at each Girl Scout meeting she found the joy to lead her daughter's troop. Yes, when she cared for her aging, sick husband as his mind started wandering away. Yes, at every week's prayer band meeting, where for over twenty years she filled the pockets of her trust with His unbroken promises. Every yes of gratitude, every yes to receive His strength, every yes that has hovered through time in her prayers for her children, for her grandchildren, for me.

The Father tells me that I can see my family history in one of two ways: it's either an unraveling account of devastation or it's a legacy of overcoming. I'm well aware of my family's pain and failures that have filtered down through generations. There have been divorces, miscarriages, clutching fears, worn-away dreams, the low-hanging shadows of shame. I *could* resent my lineage. I could place blame for my own heartaches on the brokenness handed down and remain victimized by my history, but this isn't the way God sees. Instead, He asks me to listen for the sound of legacy. This is where I've heard it: every time I visit the women of my family—sit in the living rooms of my aunts, my cousins and my own mother—the thing we do most is *laugh*. My mother has a wide, skyrocketing laugh. In her kitchen, she joyously tilts her head back and shuts her eyes; her shoulders shake, and her laughter spills freely from her chest. Somewhere dug down in the richness of its tone is the sound of what she's overcome: the anxiety, the alcoholism, the deep loneliness. She has faced her fears with the Father. Her yeses were tears I watched fall from her eyes on Sunday mornings, hands grasping a pew, as she let Jesus gently reach her saddest places. My Aunt Ida's laughter was like music, where chords of disappointment were washed by the Holy Spirit's inexplicable comfort. And my own laughter was not lost to depression, that heavy river of self-hatred that flowed through years of my life. That very river was flooded by the Father's love on the day that I let Him in; and at the shock of His kindness, all I could do was *laugh*.

The truth is, Jesus kept His scars, and so do we. They're the markings of unlikely fruit. They're the complex chords that deepen and mature our joy. I choose to see our scars as legacy, because in my family, Jesus stays close to our soil. His fingers comb the ground. Through whatever towers over us, He wants to hold the fragile flowers of our hearts. It's when we let Him that we overcome. We learn to laugh. Our legacy grows.

Prompt: Ask the Father, "In my family history, where do you see victorious legacy?" Listen, and journal His voice. Practice repentance by trading in your view of devastation for His view of beauty.

RELATING

TO DAD

Recipe for Meeting in the Middle ——— Allie Sampson

Photograph ——— Personal Collection

"How about this, Dad? You take care of planning all the nature stops, and I'll make a plan for our days in the city." I hung up the phone, my mind spilling over with coffee shop recommendations and an endless list of restaurants I wanted to try. I knew Oregon had a reputation for unbeatable waterfalls and iconic coastlines, but I was most excited about exploring Portland. This summer trip would be my first time on the West Coast, and I was determined to visit every artisan studio I followed on Instagram. I'd been quietly carrying a dream to visit the Pacific Northwest in my heart for years, and when my dad suggested we take an extravagant vacation right around my twenty-fifth birthday, my heart lit up with the promise of adventure. Together we settled on a seven-day road trip down the Oregon coast.

The idea of our adventure had me all kinds of excited, and admittedly, a little nervous. When my mom passed away six years ago, our family of three became a family of two, and soon after, my dad and I began taking short trips as a way of fighting for our connection and preserving family. We'd been on dozens of weekend getaways, but this trip was set to be the longest and the most extravagant by far. I desperately wanted it to be special, but I worried about how we'd fill our time. My dad and I have very different interests. This trip was a dream come true for both of us, but we dream really differently. For him, a West Coast adventure means full days spent at waterfalls, exploring the great outdoors. He dreams of slow hikes, interwoven with intellectual conversation and lingering off the trail to capture stunning nature photographs. I was looking forward to our time together, but I worried that navigating *how* we spent our time would leave us both feeling overwhelmed and disappointed.

The trip got off to a rocky start. A tropical storm in Florida had rerouted all flights on the East Coast just hours before our flight was supposed to leave. Long story short, my dad ended up taking three red-eye flights just to meet me in Portland. On the morning of my birthday, we loaded up in our rental car to start exploring the city, my dad exhausted from traveling through the night. Trying to handle traffic in a city we'd never been to was stressful; city driving is easily my dad's least favorite activity and navigating is not my strong suit. My underlying fear of being disappointed and my dad's lack of sleep, steeped in one of our least favorite situations to be in, was a perfect storm for disaster—and that's exactly what it was. There was panic and yelling, disappointment and crying, embarrassment and shame on both sides. Suddenly we were there—right in the middle of the moment I was terrified we'd have. Instantly, I shut down. We offered quick apologies to one another, said we forgave each other, but in reality, I struggled to let it go. This was confirmation that this trip was going to be too much. We couldn't do it. I felt defeated before we even got started.

We tried to push through and force ourselves to have fun in the city. It was miserable. We faked being happy to be there. My dad let me take the lead, trying to cater to the things he knew were important to me, but I felt the pressure to make it fun for him without actually knowing how. A few hours after lunch, we made our way to a coffee shop I'd wanted to visit and took some time to reset. I felt the temptation to hang on to my discouragement; I ordered my latte quickly, stressing over finding a seat. After I sat down, I felt the Holy Spirit pull up a stool next to me, "Hey, I want to meet you. I want to be here, and so does your dad. Don't let this moment take you out. If you give in to vulnerability and honesty here, there's a gift on the other side. I want to teach you how to relate to your dad." I took a deep breath and accepted the invitation to start over. Surrounded by strangers, my dad and I had a simple but brave communication moment. I apologized for shutting down and for freezing him out. "Dad, I really want this trip to be amazing," I confessed. "I don't want the pressure to make memories to get in the way of enjoying each other." He offered me his own honest thoughts, and within a matter of minutes we were laughing, making our way like old friends to the vintage Photo Booth in the coffee shop sitting area. We restarted our trip by taking goofy photos, each of the four frames a souvenir of our victory.

The rest of our trip was an ebb and flow of friendship. My dad let me take the lead in the city, graciously following me into independent bookstores and spending patient hours in coffee shops, reading while I water colored to my heart's content. I was surprised by how much he seemed to be enjoying himself in the city. The way I came alive in the winding aisles of books and large crowds of people invited him to see the city the way I did—full of life and hidden treasure. I caught him smiling to himself in several moments. On days spent away from the city, we explored Oregon's crowning glory: Multnomah Falls, Cannon Beach and the Columbia River Gorge. I followed my dad around unfamiliar trails and caught the same frosted-blue twinkle in his eye that he passed down to me. Surrounded by nature, I felt my own heart coming alive and thanking me for yielding to my dad's dream. It made space for me to enjoy something I would have missed. At the end of our trip, when we'd worked our way down the Oregon coast, my dad and I both stood wonder-struck together in the Redwood forest of Northern California. We both found what we were looking for: the wonder of feeling small, the wonder of being surrounded by something alive, something that masterful hands crafted. And in that moment, the relating came easily. Wonder is alive and well in my family.

Relating to our parents as an adult can be difficult. When we were very young, the relating was simpler—they toted us around on errands and many took the time to get us to little league games and dance practices. We went where they went and were taught to enjoy what they enjoyed. Now relating takes more effort. This often looks like planning, intentionality and sacrifice but sometimes, even these well-meaning things won't get us where we want to go. I believe there is an invitation for us to be vulnerable and open as adults with our parents. Learning to humble my heart and open up to my dad has required both courage and practice. I am still practicing. It is pressing, but the Lord's words ring true: "If you give in to vulnerability and honesty, there is a gift on the other side."

Prompt: Are there places in your heart that feel defeated and discouraged in trying to relate to your parents? Invite the Holy Spirit to speak into these places. Open up a specific moment to the Lord and give Him your most honest prayer. Confess where you're weary. Pray, "Father, I invite you to help me see again. Where do you have hope for my situation? Will you give me an idea of how I can relate to my parent in a new way?" Brainstorm with the Holy Spirit and write down ideas of how you can reach out to meet your parent in something they love. Initiate one or more of those ideas with your mom or dad without pressure and allow the Holy Spirit to create a new memory from a place of victory and delight.

Layers of

Significance

Recipe for Using Memory to Connect with God
Morgan Campbell

Photograph
Personal Collection

It's early August, and my family is gathered in our living room in central Georgia on a Saturday evening. We all agreed to meet together to carry on a treasured family tradition. My brother is sprawled on the floor, nestled in the nape of his husky's fur. Dad lounges behind him in folds of leather, marking his favorite spot on the family couch. I sit beside him slowing my breath, observing my family with gratitude. My mom enters carrying a sacred possession, a series of DVDs full of home footage of my childhood. Stopping to recall our lives together on the grooves of these discs has become part of the fabric of my family as we all grow older.

Mom gently loads the discs into the television, and the machine hums to motion. I immediately enter into a world that feels far away, yet wildly familiar. Small, in-between moments that I assumed had fallen into the crack of time begin to unravel layers of significance and identity in my heart. I see my dad, so young and able, instructing me to carve open the top of a pumpkin and scoop out the seeds. I smell the air of my nursery on Winchester Street as my mom's blonde curls bop into the room and soothe my sleepy eyes. I feel the clear, salty waves kiss my toes as they crash onto the shore of the Florida coast. I watch my parents take turns videotaping our birthday parties, while the other one wipes icing from my face. I hear my grandmother's voice telling me who I am, loving me through tears and laughter.

As a single, young adult in my twenties, it's been really valuable to create rhythms of celebrating family. I've not always been able to appreciate the magic of these moments, but over time I have learned how to stop and ask the Holy Spirit to help me see my upbringing through His eyes. This practice of perspective has slowly turned any of my youthful angst and confusion into a settling of gratitude and compassion. Watching these old home videos leaves me with deep reverence for each person that invested time and energy into my life. They have opened up elbow room in my heart for my parents to be human, real and imperfect as I see them at twenty-five—the age I am now—giving all that they knew how to give. In my youth, I couldn't consciously receive the gift of my dad's presence or my mom's comfort. Reliving these moments as an adult is like opening the gift a second time and discovering another hidden layer of goodness. By recording the simple moments of my life, my parents were unknowingly saying, "Morgan, your life is valuable and worth documenting." I let my heart fill with an ocean's worth of gratitude at my beautiful, ordinary and profound life.

Whether you have hundreds of hours of footage from your childhood or a few pictures, we all possess one of the greatest gifts God gave us: memory. Memory allows us to enter into our imagination and unearth treasure from the past. The magic of these home videos helps me realize that the Lord Himself has been recording and documenting simple moments my whole life long. He can replay and enjoy them any time; He does not forget our stories. God has the ability to teach us about ourselves and bring significance to our humanity. The substance of memory is deep and beautiful; it sails on the waves of time and offers itself to those who call upon it. It shakes hands with our lives and reminds us that we are valuable to God and worthy of remembrance.

Prompt: Invite the Holy Spirit to highlight some of His favorite memories from your childhood. In your journal, ask Him, "Lord, why do these memories matter to you? How have these memories positively affected me in my adult life?" Once you've journaled His voice, choose a scene or object from that memory and sketch or paint it in your journal.

Back Where I Started

Recipe for Celebrating Your Parents ——— *Molly Skaggs*

Photograph ——— *Personal Collection*

In the process of making my first album last year, I invited my family to be a part of the recording. We had the incredible privilege of working at my dad's music studio for a few days in Tennessee. I asked Dad to play on a song I wrote called *Back Where I Started*. My desire was two-fold: firstly, I wanted my parents to be connected to my life and music; secondly, I wanted to connect my listeners to my family's heritage by giving my parents space to be themselves within my own music. I live away from my parents now, and the path I've chosen musically is different from theirs. My deepest desire was to share my most authentic sound by honoring where I came from— from them! While I was excited, I admit there was a bit of hesitation in asking Dad to play. I began to wonder, "What if he doesn't understand or feels awkward? What if this brings anxiety rather than the harmony I desire?" Nevertheless, I moved against the fear and pursued my dad. Having him sit in the seat of honor within this particular song was the most important thing to me.

The song arrangement was crafted with space for him to play a style of old-time fiddle that's quite special to me called "Triple Fiddles." It's a sound I've heard him play since I was a little girl. I watched him while he tracked the song, bent over with his fiddle and bow, making the sweet, familiar sounds of home. Soft, quiet tears welled up in my eyes as I was caught up in a moment where Heaven's vaults of honor were opened. I began to really see and remember all the collected moments of my dad's celebration of me throughout my life. The Father began to whisper the truth to my heart. He showed me how my desire to connect with my dad through sound only reflected my dad's original desire to connect with me throughout my entire life.

My parents celebrating me throughout my life was their way of marking me every day with an affirming, "I love you. I'm proud of you. My life is more beautiful because you are in it, and I wouldn't have it any other way." I remembered as a young girl sitting on the couch with my dad in my childhood home singing Paul McCartney's harmony parts to his John Lennon lead and guitar in their song *Help!* I felt the warmth of his heart to spend time with me. I remembered singing and playing countless stages where, standing by his side, Dad's face beamed with the delight of a very proud father. I remembered every one of my band concerts, piano recitals and church programs he attended, cheering louder than anyone. I was born from the rich soil of simple, everyday celebration; I grew in it as a seedling and am now becoming a mighty oak. These consistent celebratory moments not only shaped my life as a musician, but as a daughter. And now, these moments resurfaced, all leading up to this momentous occasion.

In the studio my heart overflowed with thanksgiving, for there he was—my master musician father—offering his absolute best to make my own music shine. The recording session required hard work, but Dad never ceased to give his whole heart. When we wrapped up for the day, I found myself full to the brim with gratitude. "Dad, thank you so much for all that you did today!" I smiled, my arms squeezing around him as I have always done since I was small. "Honey, you are so welcome. This was great! I can hardly believe that this happened today…a long time coming!" he beamed, squeezing back, his cheek resting on my head. "This meant so much to me, Dad. It is only right to have you on my first album. You shaped me. Your heart is woven into every single one of these songs, because your sound is in me. Everyone is going to hear where I come from, and I'm thankful for it. That, and no one plays fiddle like you! You have always been my favorite," I replied, pouring the fullness of my heart back to him.

Celebrating my Dad that day meant doing for him what he has done for me all my life. He first risked vulnerability by inviting me into his world of music and what he loved, never really knowing if I would understand or want to connect there; but our shared love for music reinforced our connection throughout my life and became a meeting place of growth and friendship with him as I learned from one of the very best. Now, I had the opportunity to celebrate him by opening up my own world and inviting him to experience the beauty and strength of his sound in me. Honor and celebration gave way for a deeper connection with my dad. It was my own way of marking him as his daughter and friend with an affirming, "I love you. I'm proud of you. My life is more beautiful because you are in it, and I wouldn't have it any other way." The honor we give to our parents is coming into agreement with the Father's own delight over them. Celebration of a parent helps continue a legacy of building strong families in every generation who can become mighty oaks. It forges value into every human heart and seals in their worth. By going back to where we started and nourishing our roots, we can give life to our entire family tree.

Prompt: Pray to the Father, "What are some simple ways I can celebrate my parents in this season of our lives as both their child and friend? Lord, open up doors for moments where I can see and offer them my gratitude for who they are to me." Journal His response to you; then go nourish your roots! Write a short card or letter to your mom and/or dad celebrating who they are to you. Mail it expecting nothing in return. Feel the Father's delight in you as you share your appreciation with your parents.

age 1.5

age 11

age 4

Neal, age 11 + Martha, age 8

Inheritance

Recipe for Valuing What You've Been Given ———— Martha McRae
Photography ———— Personal Collection

"Whatever you do, work at it with all your heart, as working for the Lord, not for human masters, since you know that you will receive an inheritance from the Lord as a reward. It is the Lord Christ you are serving" (Colossians 3:23-24, NIV).

My parents raised my brother and me in the country, outside of a small North Carolina farming community. On top of devoting their lives to farming, they both have dedicated four decades to managing their own businesses. They are driven and unified, fluidly moving back and forth to help each other in work and family. Sustainable agriculture has always run deep in my family's blood, and growing acres of vegetables and fruit to provide food for the entire year was our "normal." You name it, we grew it: squash, zucchini, potatoes, tomatoes. The list goes on. Summer break to me meant tending to our enormous garden together under the rays of the hot sun.

Every year, when the time came to harvest our green bean crop, we would wake up with the sun to pick. Sitting on upside-down five-gallon buckets, we would slowly inch our way down the 200-foot rows of vines, filling and dragging bushel baskets with us until they were full to the brim with fresh green beans. When the heat of the day would become unbearable, we would tiredly make our way inside our house for cool showers and lunch—usually a satisfying banana-mayonnaise sandwich. The afternoon and evening would be spent snapping, cleaning and canning the morning's harvest, while watching the original Star Wars Trilogy on VHS. The next morning, we would do it all over again.

When I was a kid, I struggled with feeling like I was missing out when the other kids would play all summer long. I didn't understand the scope of what we were doing, growing our family's food for the year. I had a bad attitude and complained a lot; when the sweat is rolling down your face and your clothes are covered in dirt, it's hard to be grateful. However, as an adult, I look back at those hot summer days and appreciate the gift of hard work that was given to me. Work is beautiful. The Trinity created man to work with Him, to name the animals and tend the land in Eden. The Father knew that we would not only *need*, but actually *desire* to labor in order to achieve something great and purposeful. He knew that we would come alive when we get down in the dirt, just as He did when He breathed life into us. He created us like Himself.

I've inherited the value of hard work from my parents; they taught me by their own example. An inheritance is passed on from one generation to the next, and given the chance, it has the possibility to grow, to be refined and to become stronger. I've had the privilege of being parented by two salt-of-the-earth people, who let divinely-inspired value lead our family. Beyond the generations of farmers that precede me, hard work has become a life-long value to me. When I work hard unto the Lord, I see the Father's intentionality bringing me closer to Him again and again. As we lead schools and internships year round at A Place for the Heart, the value of hard work is something I pass along to every student. Whether it's teaching someone how to cook or how to care for the grounds, I am consistently imparting the value of tending. Hard work rooted in Jesus' belovedness is the inheritance I now give.

Prompt: Ask the Lord, "What is one God-given trait or quality that my parents have passed down to me? How can I continue cultivating this value in my life now and impart it to others?" Listen, and journal His response.

I AM FOUGHT FOR

Recipe for Giving Back through Encouragement ——— Allie Sampson
Cedar Woodcut, approx. 63 years old ——— Morgan Campbell

My dad, Rusty, is one of the most inspiring people I know. He is six feet of tall wisdom, with a salt-and-pepper beard and twinkling blue eyes. He wears surprisingly trendy glasses for a former sports coach in his early sixties and balances a full schedule as a pastor, teacher and assistant athletic director for the local high school. He is the perfect mix of practicality and humor—equally as quick to make a strategy and a joke. He loves maps, a good campfire, Ethiopian coffee and compelling conversation.

My dad and I are very close. Transitioning into adulthood has given me eyes to see how truly remarkable of a man he is. In my late teen years, it was easy to identify and complain about the lack I perceived in my parenting—the things that I never learned or was taught. The gaps seemed obvious, and it was easier to complain and make excuses about the deficit than reconcile it. This experience is not exclusive to me. We were all raised by humans—people who, just like us, have stories, histories, hurts and lack of their own.

As I became an adult and invited the Lord into my perspective of my parents, I began to be filled with compassion and gratitude for them. In my own effort to navigate early adulthood, I began to understand why they made some of the choices they did.

My dad grew up without a father. At the tender age of nine years old, his dad passed away, and Rusty became the man of the house. The years leading up to his father's passing left him with difficult memories. His own parenting deficit was deep—the loss and lack were significant. He did not have the privilege of seeing how fathers connect with their children. He wasn't taught how to connect with his daughter. This was something he grappled with in the early years of parenting and diligently fought to understand. Years upon years dedicated to learning fatherly pursuit. It took time and effort, but to both our benefit, he chose to learn. He overcame tremendous odds when he became a committed father; showing up to every church play, choir concert and cheerleading competition. He made a point to be what his own dad never could be: present.

I watched him go on a journey of transformation—in fact, I was a companion on that journey. As family, we journey together, regardless of how intentionally we choose to. When my dad started down the path of intentional fatherhood, I was the one he carried as he walked.

The great privilege of life in God is that we get to become what we never received. I see this truth playing out in my dad every time he offers me a compliment, calls me just to say hello and initiates making the six-hour drive to have a weekend together. There are so many places where he filled the gaps in our generational line so that I wouldn't have to. Shoveling heaps of *I am proud of you* and *You are worth my time* into the foundations of our family history.

Recently I was thinking of my dad, the work he's put in to change our family line. I was moved. It was mid-October, right in the middle of my busiest season. We were hosting our two-month discipleship school where our team puts in long days of leading, teaching and counseling our students. During sessions, I'd find myself overwhelmed with gratitude for my dad, having memories of times where he went the distance to connect with me or offer me things he did not directly receive from his own parents. I knew his birthday was coming up, and I wanted to do something special for him. Instead of getting overwhelmed by the tension of adding another thing to my to-do list, I simply invited the Lord to help me find a way to communicate what I wanted to say.

A few days later on a Sabbath day, I was plunking simple notes out on my ukulele. I don't play often, but in that season, it was how I engaged creativity and connection with the Lord in a restful way. Strumming through old favorites and some songs I'd written in earlier seasons, I found a new chord progression rising to the surface. All of a sudden a simple thought resonated in my spirit, *What if you wrote your dad a song for his birthday?* My eyes widened and a smile stretched across my face. *Yes, Holy Spirit. I love that idea! Will you give me a song for my dad?*

I sat on my deck, eyes closed, finger-picking the same progression over and over again. As I relaxed into the melody, sacred memories welled up from deep places. My earliest memory of quality time with my dad, catching tree-frogs in our back yard. My most recent memory of time spent journaling and watercoloring together in a coffee shop. The collection of things he's taught me: how to play Crazy Eights, give a firm handshake, change my car battery, turn off the anxious thoughts one by one when I cannot fall asleep. Without realizing it, I was humming and suddenly, lyrics formed. Verses about the beginning of our connection to how we relate now. A chorus of celebrating feeling safe and at home. And a bridge that effortlessly rose up from deep gratitude and swirled through the autumn air:

> *"And one day I'll pass down*
> *all the things that I am proud*
> *to say I learned from my dad.*
>
> *I am proud to call you mine.*
> *Thank you for this happy life*
> *that you worked so hard to build."*

Those lyrics overflowed from the pride I feel in my soul to be my father's daughter. The overwhelming gratitude for his choices, the consideration of all his quiet decisions, the weight of the big and small moments that led to me being able to confidently say, *I have a very present father*, collided in a glorious hour of crafting, writing and singing. It was that simple. The next evening, on my dad's sixty-first birthday, I called him through FaceTime and played him the song he'd inspired me to write. When I reached the bridge, tears filled both our eyes. The profound truth of those simple words resonated in both of our souls. Tears of hard-won victory streamed down our faces. I sang it again and we both felt the weight. Together we celebrated the life he's built.

Prompt: Have you been so focused on the deficits in your family story that you've missed your parents' victories? Invite the Holy Spirit to fill you with honor, compassion and gratitude for your parents. Sit and receive His thoughts over them. From a place of compassion and gratitude, collect your thoughts and choose one of the following ways to share your thankfulness with them:

1)   If you are moved by imagery, write your parents a poem. If you're musical and enjoy songwriting, craft your thoughts into a song. Enjoy writing with the Father, celebrating your parents who are so special to Him. Once the poem or song is complete, make time to share it them, either in person or over Skype or FaceTime.

2)   Is your heart overflowing with thoughts? Write your parents a letter. Intentionally explore your gratitude and savor the process of capturing it on paper. Find a time to sit your parents down and read your letter to them in person. If you live far away, mail it to them.

THE CAGELESS BIRDS

"We escaped like a bird from a hunter's trap. The trap is broken, and we are free!" Psalm 124:7, NLT

The Cageless Birds is a community of leaders and artisans from Sophia, North Carolina founded by Jonathan and Melissa Helser. We are drawn together by an authentic passion for the gospel of Jesus and a commitment to live out wholeness in community. We believe in the risk of saying yes to flying out of the cage of fear and soaring on the wings of true identity. We have fallen in love with pouring out our lives in ministry and then refilling our hearts in rhythms of family, friendship and creativity. This is sustainability. This is what it means to fly high and build home.

As leaders, we believe in and are committed to seeing a generation transformed by the Gospel. This commitment is walked out through our discipleship school, The 18 Inch Journey. Here, we set a table for students from around the world to come and encounter the love of the Father, the power of the Cross, the sustainability of the Holy Spirit, and the beautiful transformation that happens in community.

As artisans, we come alive in creating goods throughout the year that help support our growing families and the mission of our schools. Whether it's creating music, writing books or cultivating one of our many other art forms, we are anchored with joy in the pursuit of excellence in all that we do.

For more on the Cageless Birds, visit our website and online store at *cagelessbirds.com*.

2018 CONTRIBUTORS

THE CAGELESS BIRDS

JONATHAN DAVID HELSER

MELISSA HELSER

KEN HELSER

LINDA HELSER

JUSTINA STEVENS

JAKE STEVENS

JD GRAVITT

ERIN GRAVITT

CHRIS MILLER

JESSIE MILLER

JOEL CASE

KATELAND CASE

MOLLY SKAGGS

MARTHA MCRAE

LUKE SKAGGS

ROSEMARY SKAGGS

LINDSAY VANCE

ZAC VANCE

ALLIE SAMPSON

PHYLLIS UNKEFER

SYDNEE MELA

MORGAN CAMPBELL

FRIENDS OF THE CAGELESS BIRDS

DAVID BURBACH
Winston-Salem, North Carolina
motherfathermag.com

BETHANY DOUGLASS
Bryan, Texas
cloisteredaway.com

MATT & DEBBIE PETERSON
Winston-Salem, North Carolina
awakechurch.com

MARTIN & ANNA SMITH
Brighton, England
martinsmith.tv

BLAKE & SHANNON CASTEEL
Kona, Hawaii
respectthecorners.com

SEAN & KATE FEUCHT
Redding, California
seanfeucht.com

KATIE RIDDLE
Redding, California
riddlelove.com

RITA SPRINGER
Hurst, Texas
ritaspringer.com

HAVILAH CUNNINGTON
Redding, California
havilahcunnington.com

PETE & SAMMY GREIG
Guildford, England
24-7prayer.com

STEPHEN & SARAH ROACH
Greensboro, North Carolina
stephenroach.org

JASON & RACHEL UPTON
Milwaukee, Wisconsin
jasonupton.com

JASON & LAUREN VALLOTTON
Redding, California
bethel.com

THE CULTIVATE COLLECTION

Discover all the volumes of the Cultivate Collection at cagelessbirds.com.

I. THE HEAD TO HEART JOURNEY

An introduction to journaling with the Lord, featuring prompts and writings on topics from enjoying God and savoring your life, to freedom and identity. This book was created to help you establish rhythms of conversation with God.

II. THE CLARITY WINTER BRINGS

Designed to help you find beauty in quieter seasons of the heart, this book includes writings on topics such as hope, patience, perspective and stillness and is meant to encourage you to hear His voice in the midst of bare seasons.

III. FLY HIGH. BUILD HOME.

Created to bring understanding to what it means to thrive and live a sustainable life, this volume will explore what it means to thrive—to soar in the seemingly mundane moments of your life as well as the big-picture occasions.

IV. CREATIVITY UNLOCKED

Words and prompts that empower you to take risks in expression and discover your creative ability. These writings are meant to challenge your idea of what creativity is and unlock the truth that creativity is a birthright, not a skill-set.

V. THE ART OF CONNECTION, PT. I

Written with your most significant relationships in mind, Volume V is designed to encourage and empower you to pursue healthy and thriving relationships in dating, marriage, parenting and relating to your parents. May these writings inspire you with courage, hope and healthy perspective for God-centered relationships with those who mean the most to you.

EDITOR IN CHIEF
Melissa Helser

ART DIRECTION AND GRAPHIC DESIGN
Melissa Helser, Justina Stevens, Lindsay Vance & Morgan Campbell

COPY EDITORS
Sarah Roach, Courtney Clark, Allie Sampson, Erin Gravitt
Justina Stevens & Phyllis Unkefer

Cover Photograph by Melissa Helser

Section Paintings by Justina Stevens

Handlettered titles and type by Lindsay Vance

PERSONAL COLLECTION PHOTOGRAPHY
Everyday Forgiveness - Alex Douglas
Values the Transcend Circumstances - Anna Naphtali
All My Sons - Adam Mowery
Honest and Open - Elle Limebear
An Obedient Yes - Jon Volk
Through the Fire - Vivienne Marcheel
The Priority is Connection - Heather Armstrong

BIBLIOGRAPHY
1 *Zach Brittle, LMHC. "Turn Towards Instead of Away." The Gottman Relationship Blog, 1 Apr. 2015, https://www.gottman.com/blog/turn-toward-instead-of-away/.*
2 *Manning, Brennan. The Furious Longing of God. David C. Cook, 2009.*
3 *Youssef, Michael. "Call Upon the Lord." Leading The Way with Dr. Michael Youssef, 30 Mar. 2016, www.ltw.org/read/my-devotional/2016/03/call-upon-the-lord.*
4 *Henry David Thoreau." AZQuotes.com. Wind and Fly LTD, 05 April 2018, http://www.azquotes.com/quote/344197.*
5 *Palacio, R. J. Wonder. W. Ross MacDonald School Resource Services Library, 2015.*
6 *Shakespeare, William, and George Richard Hibbard. Hamlet. Oxford University Press, 2008. Act 5, Scene 2.*
7 *Scazzero, Peter. "The 25 EHS Truisms * Emotionally Healthy Spirituality." Emotionally Healthy Spirituality, 25 Oct. 2016, www.emotionallyhealthy.org/25-ehs-truisms/.*
8 *Ilachinski, Andy. "'Chance Favors the Prepared Mind.'" Tao of Photography, 13 July 2007, tao-of-digital-photography.blogspot.com/2007/07/chance-favors-prepared-mind.html.*

All definitions are quoted from the Merriam-Webster.com dictionary, 2018
All section Scriptures are from the NIV translation.

CONNECT + SUPPORT

VISIT OUR STORE
cagelessbirds.com
to purchase copies, handcrafted goods
and to read our blog

INSTAGRAM
@cagelessbirds

DISCIPLESHIP RETREATS AND SCHOOLS
18inchjourney.com

WHOLESALE & QUESTIONS
cagelessbirdsstore@gmail.com